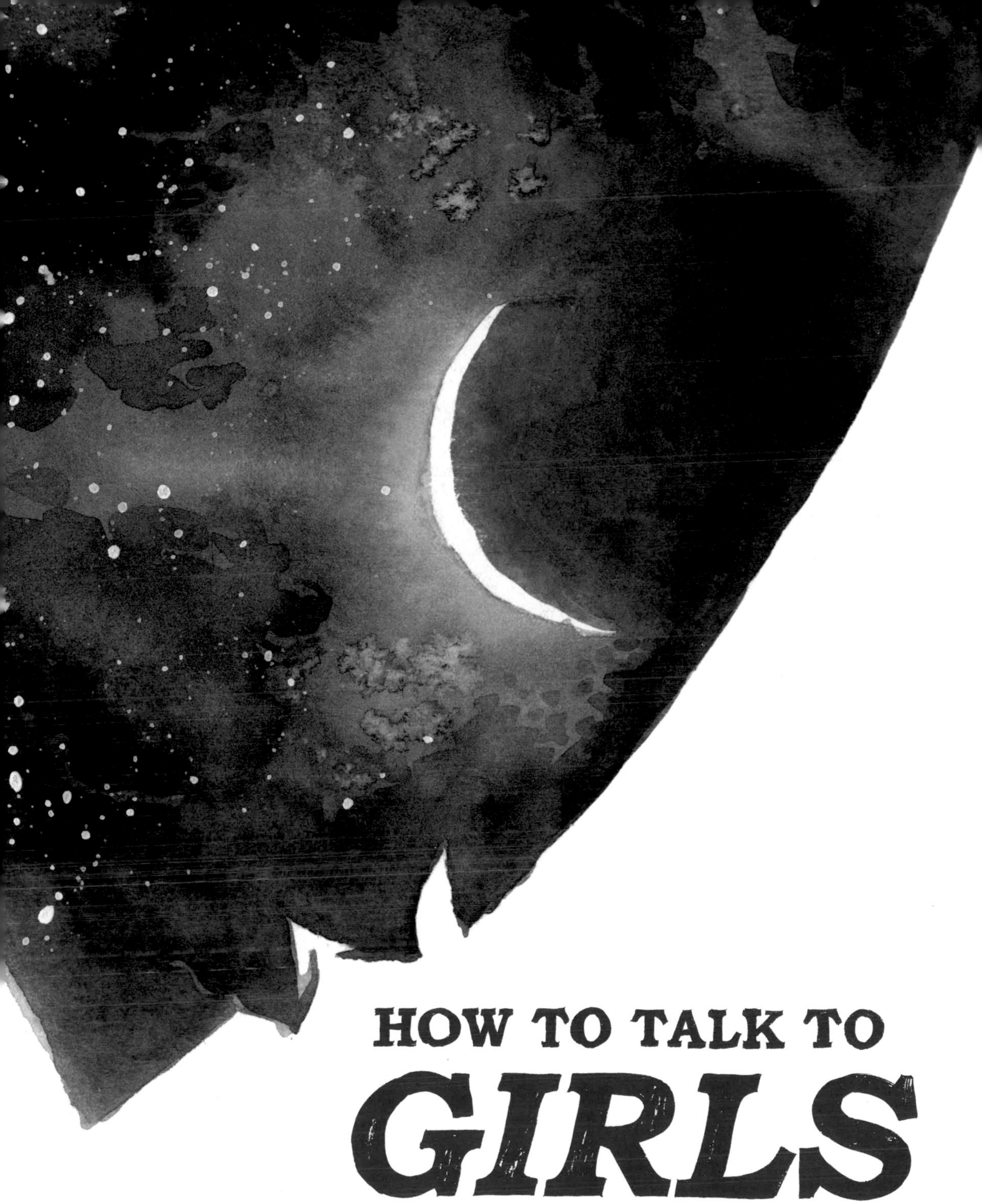

HOW TO TALK TO GIRLS AT PARTIES

by

Neil Gaiman

adaptation, art, & lettering by

Fábio Moon & Gabriel Bá

Dark Horse Books

Based on the short story "How to Talk to Girls at Parties"
by Neil Gaiman, originally published in *Fragile Things* (2006).

Published by Dark Horse Books
A division of Dark Horse Comics, Inc.
10956 SE Main Street
Milwaukie, Oregon 97222

DarkHorse.com

First edition: June 2016
ISBN 978-1-61655-955-7

1 3 5 7 9 10 8 6 4 2
Printed in China

Library of Congress Cataloging-in-Publication Data

Names: Gaiman, Neil, author. | Bá, Gabriel, illustrator. | Moon, Fábio, illustrator.
Title: How to talk to girls at parties / by Neil Gaiman ; adaptation, art, &
lettering by Fábio Moon and Gabriel Bá.
Description: First edition. | Milwaukie, OR : Dark Horse Books, 2016.
Identifiers: LCCN 2015050695 | ISBN 9781616559557 (hardback)
Subjects: LCSH: Graphic novels. | Comic books, strips, etc. | BISAC: COMICS &
GRAPHIC NOVELS / Fantasy.
Classification: LCC PN6727.G35 H69 2016 | DDC 741.5/942--dc23
LC record available at http://lccn.loc.gov/2015050695

Publisher
Mike Richardson

Editor
Diana Schutz

Associate Editor
Aaron Walker

Designer and Digital Art Technician
Cary Grazzini

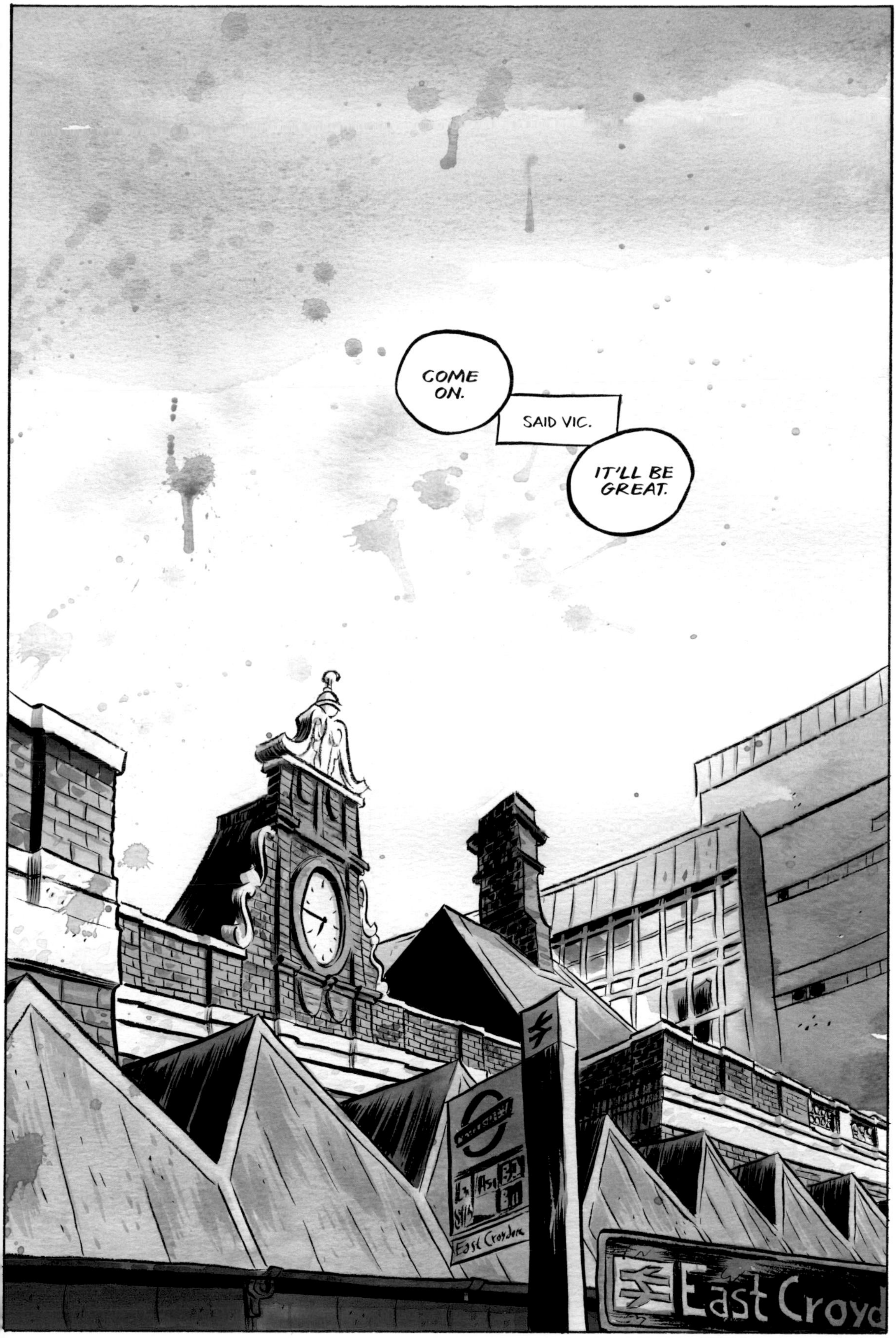
COME ON.
SAID VIC.
IT'LL BE GREAT.
East Croydon
East Croyd

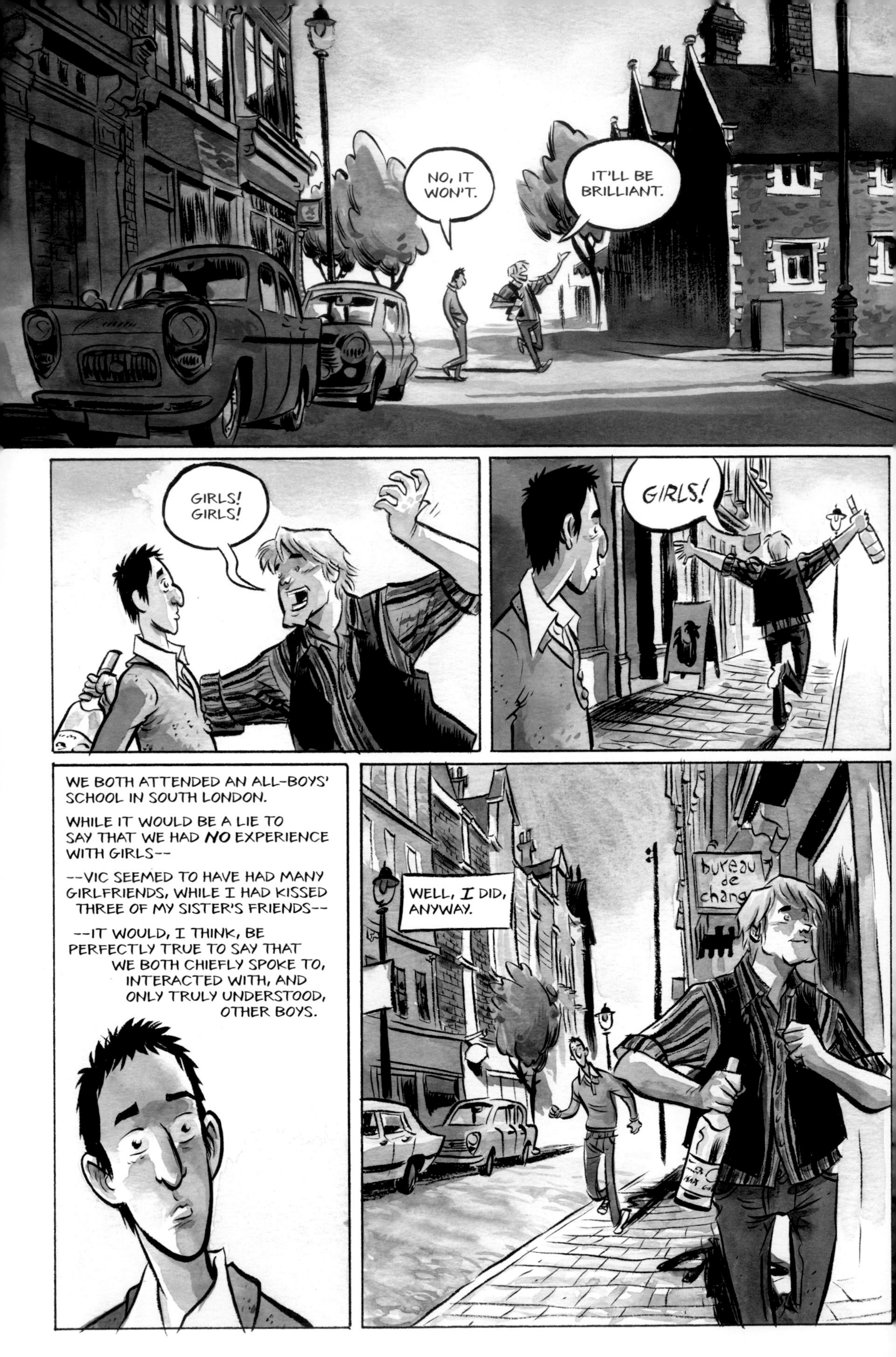
NO, IT WON'T.
IT'LL BE BRILLIANT.
GIRLS! GIRLS!
GIRLS!
WE BOTH ATTENDED AN ALL-BOYS' SCHOOL IN SOUTH LONDON.
WHILE IT WOULD BE A LIE TO SAY THAT WE HAD NO EXPERIENCE WITH GIRLS--
--VIC SEEMED TO HAVE HAD MANY GIRLFRIENDS, WHILE I HAD KISSED THREE OF MY SISTER'S FRIENDS--
--IT WOULD, I THINK, BE PERFECTLY TRUE TO SAY THAT WE BOTH CHIEFLY SPOKE TO, INTERACTED WITH, AND ONLY TRULY UNDERSTOOD, OTHER BOYS.
WELL, I DID, ANYWAY.
bureau de chang

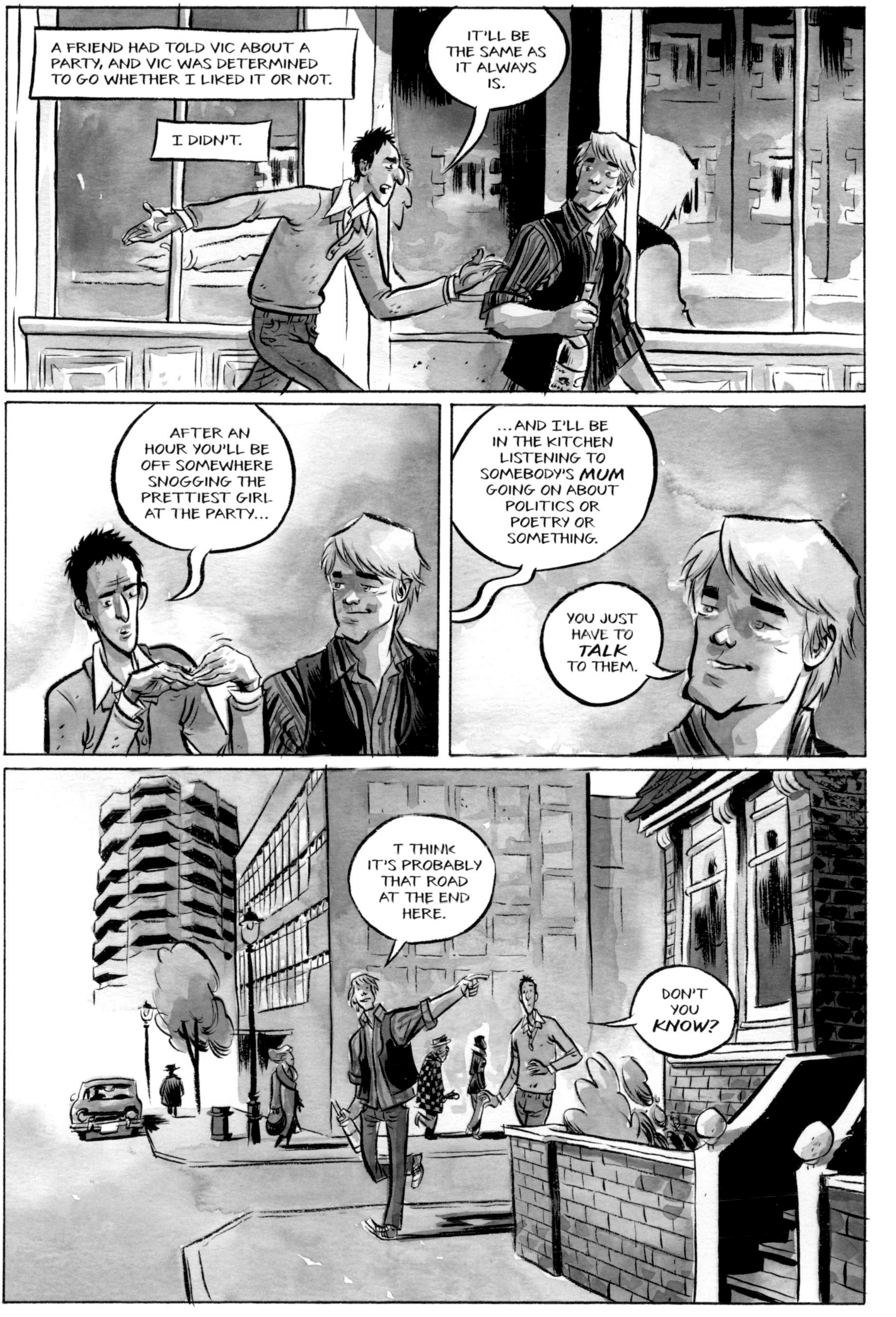
A FRIEND HAD TOLD VIC ABOUT A PARTY, AND VIC WAS DETERMINED TO GO WHETHER I LIKED IT OR NOT.
IT'LL BE THE SAME AS IT ALWAYS IS.
I DIDN'T.
AFTER AN HOUR YOU'LL BE OFF SOMEWHERE SNOGGING THE PRETTIEST GIRL AT THE PARTY...
...AND I'LL BE IN THE KITCHEN LISTENING TO SOMEBODY'S MUM GOING ON ABOUT POLITICS OR POETRY OR SOMETHING.
YOU JUST HAVE TO TALK TO THEM.
I THINK IT'S PROBABLY THAT ROAD AT THE END HERE.
DON'T YOU KNOW?

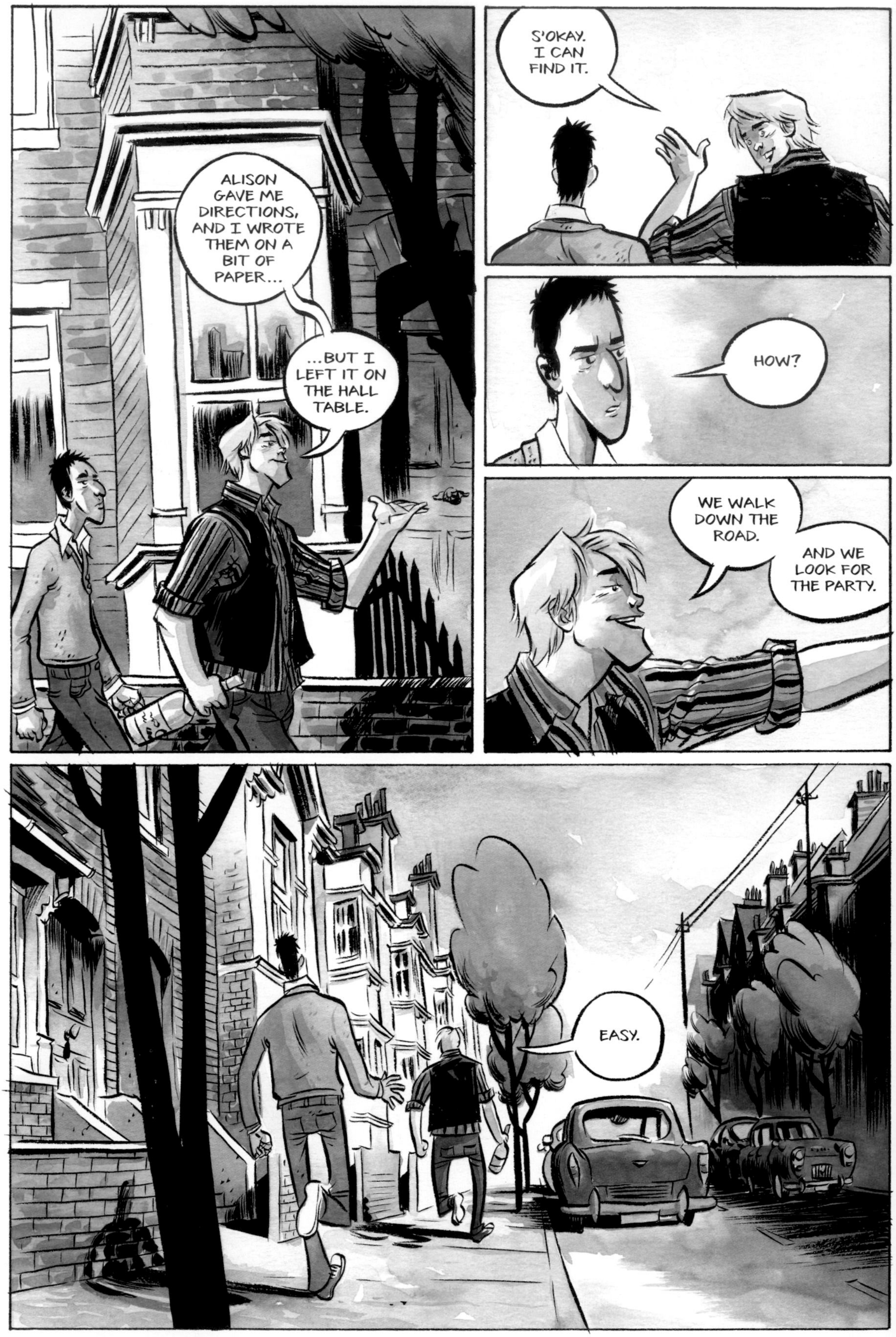
ALISON GAVE ME DIRECTIONS, AND I WROTE THEM ON A BIT OF PAPER...
...BUT I LEFT IT ON THE HALL TABLE.
S'OKAY. I CAN FIND IT.
HOW?
WE WALK DOWN THE ROAD.
AND WE LOOK FOR THE PARTY.
EASY.

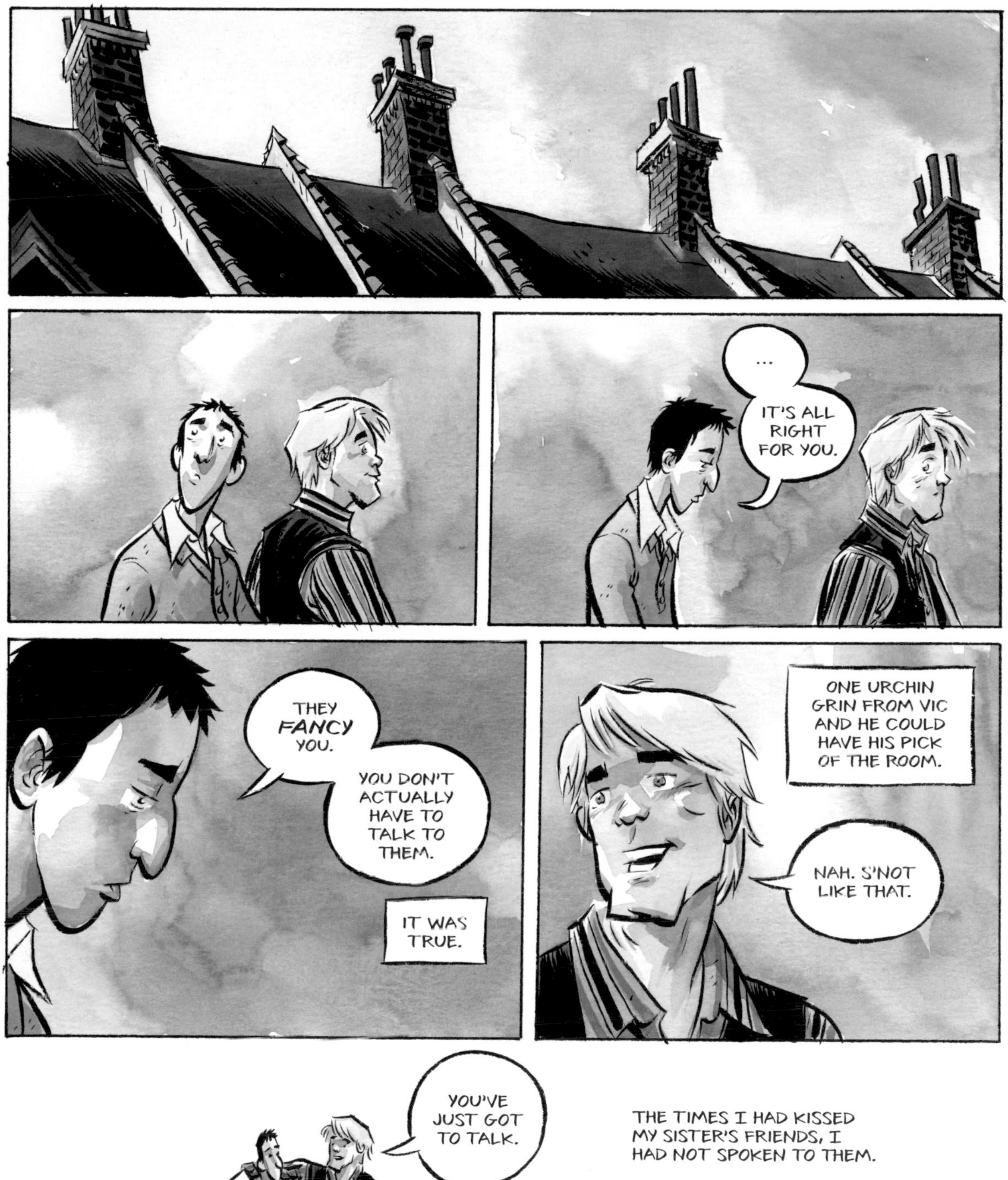
...
IT'S ALL RIGHT FOR YOU.
THEY FANCY YOU.
YOU DON'T ACTUALLY HAVE TO TALK TO THEM.
IT WAS TRUE.
ONE URCHIN GRIN FROM VIC AND HE COULD HAVE HIS PICK OF THE ROOM.
NAH. S'NOT LIKE THAT.
YOU'VE JUST GOT TO TALK.
THE TIMES I HAD KISSED MY SISTER'S FRIENDS, I HAD NOT SPOKEN TO THEM.
THEY HAD BEEN AROUND WHILE MY SISTER WAS OFF DOING SOMETHING ELSEWHERE, AND THEY HAD DRIFTED INTO MY ORBIT, AND SO I HAD KISSED THEM.
I DO NOT REMEMBER ANY TALKING.

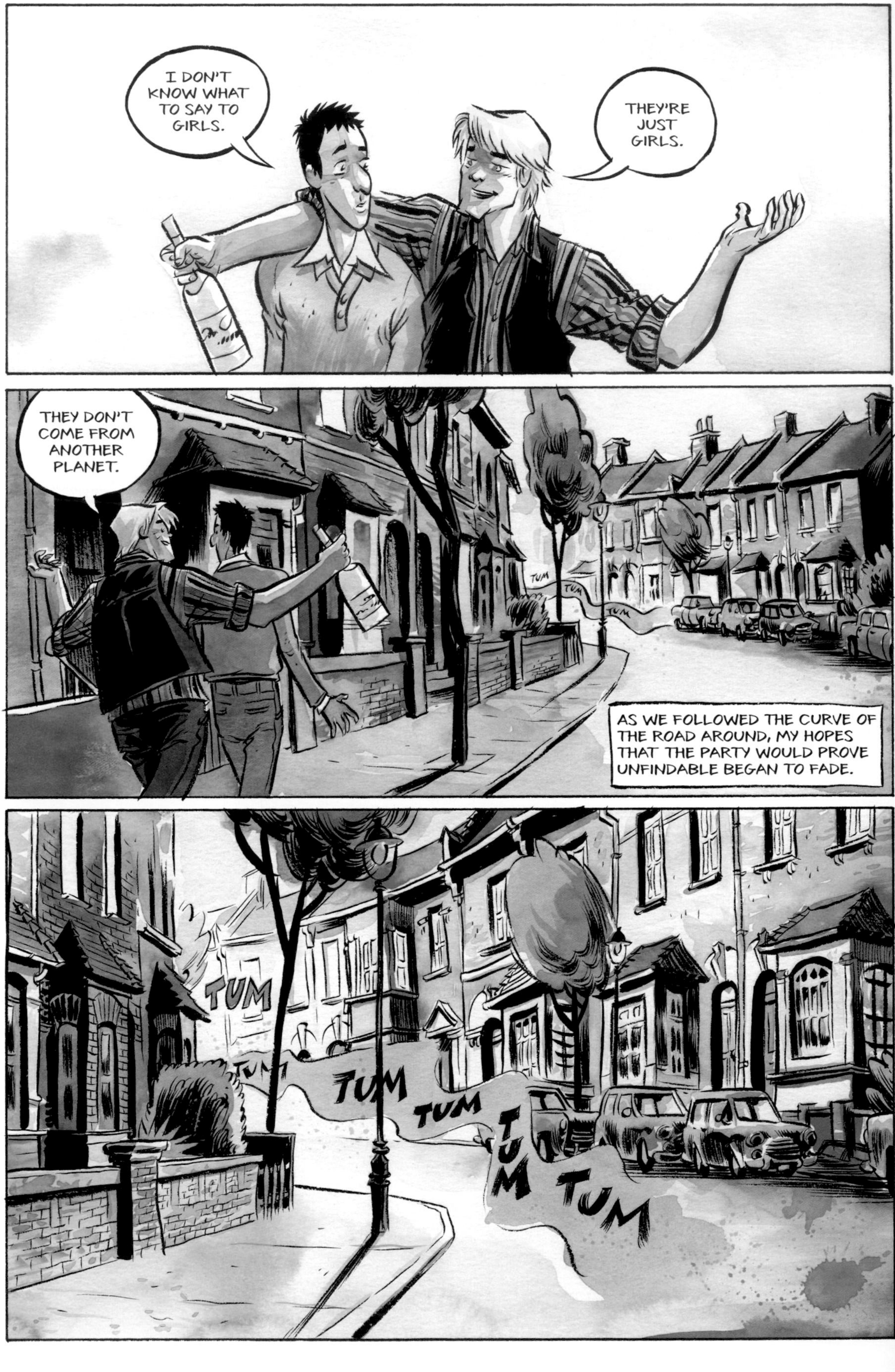
I DON'T KNOW WHAT TO SAY TO GIRLS.
THEY'RE JUST GIRLS.
THEY DON'T COME FROM ANOTHER PLANET.
TUM TUM TUM
AS WE FOLLOWED THE CURVE OF THE ROAD AROUND, MY HOPES THAT THE PARTY WOULD PROVE UNFINDABLE BEGAN TO FADE.
TUM TUM TUM TUM TUM TUM

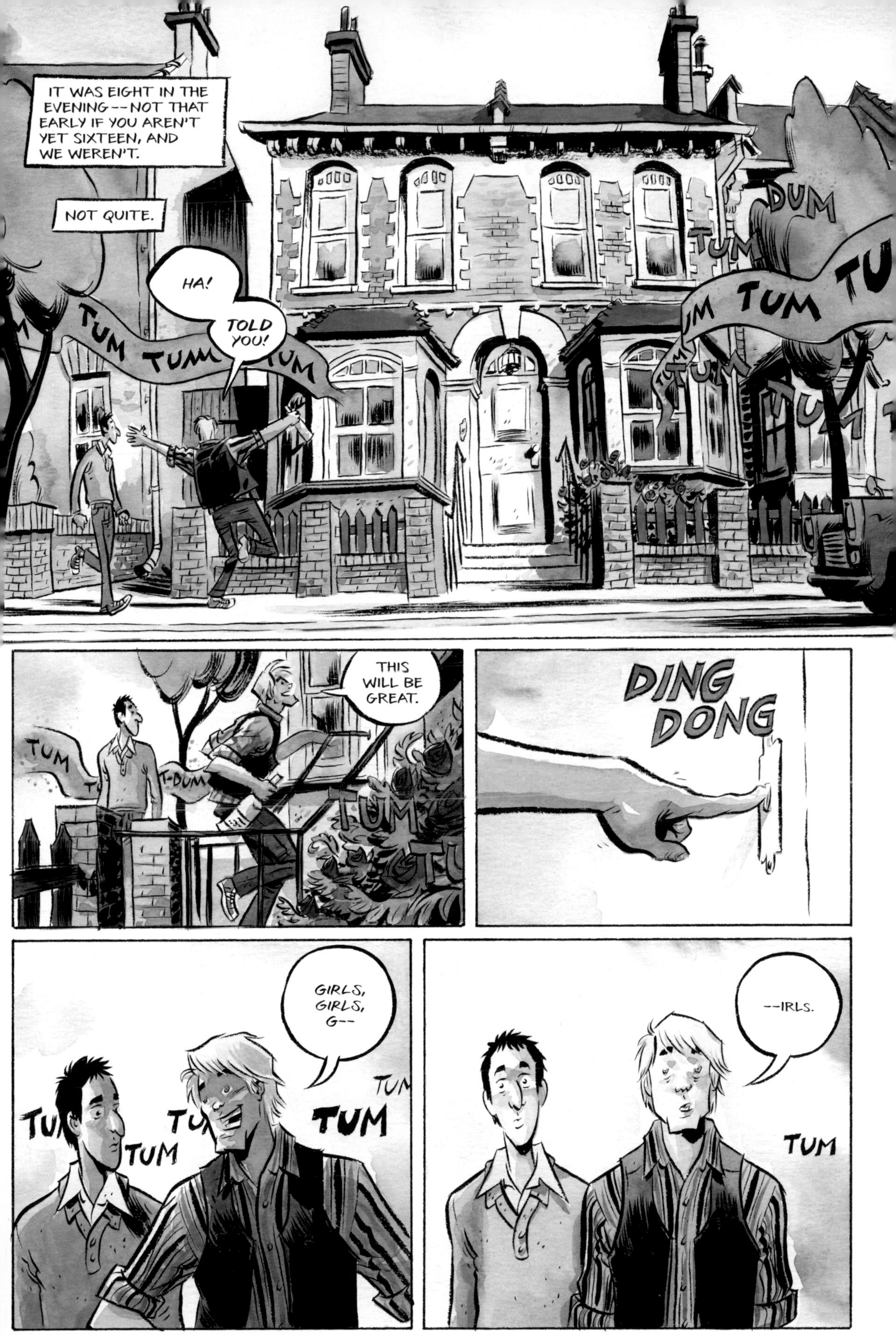
IT WAS EIGHT IN THE EVENING--NOT THAT EARLY IF YOU AREN'T YET SIXTEEN, AND WE WEREN'T.
NOT QUITE.
DUM
TUM
TUM TUM TUM
TUM TUM TUM
HA!
TOLD YOU!
THIS WILL BE GREAT.
TUM
T-DUM
TUM
DING DONG
GIRLS, GIRLS, G--
TUM
TUM
TUM
TUM
--IRLS.
TUM

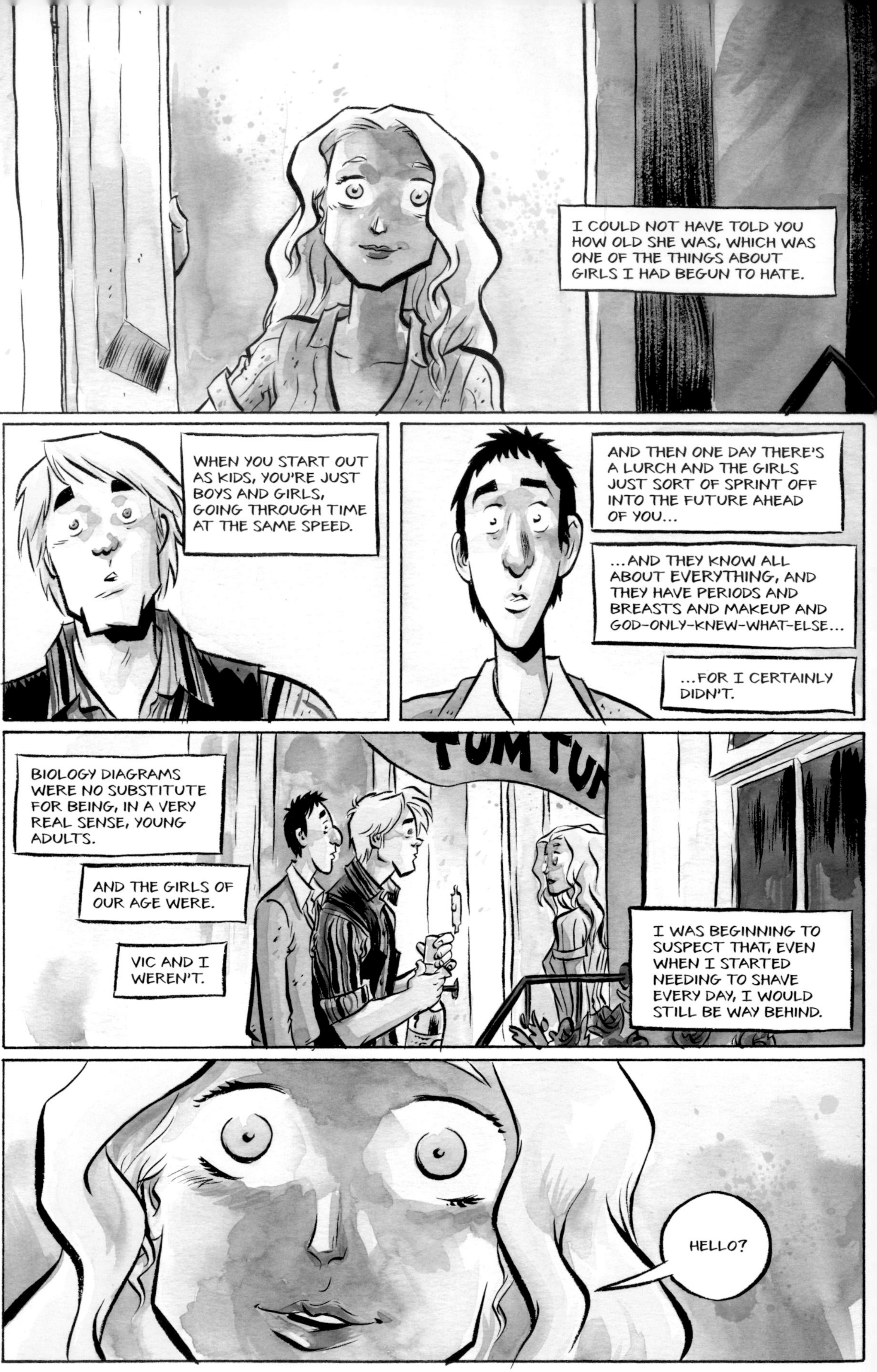
I COULD NOT HAVE TOLD YOU HOW OLD SHE WAS, WHICH WAS ONE OF THE THINGS ABOUT GIRLS I HAD BEGUN TO HATE.
WHEN YOU START OUT AS KIDS, YOU'RE JUST BOYS AND GIRLS, GOING THROUGH TIME AT THE SAME SPEED.
AND THEN ONE DAY THERE'S A LURCH AND THE GIRLS JUST SORT OF SPRINT OFF INTO THE FUTURE AHEAD OF YOU...
...AND THEY KNOW ALL ABOUT EVERYTHING, AND THEY HAVE PERIODS AND BREASTS AND MAKEUP AND GOD-ONLY-KNEW-WHAT-ELSE...
...FOR I CERTAINLY DIDN'T.
BIOLOGY DIAGRAMS WERE NO SUBSTITUTE FOR BEING, IN A VERY REAL SENSE, YOUNG ADULTS.
AND THE GIRLS OF OUR AGE WERE.
VIC AND I WEREN'T.
I WAS BEGINNING TO SUSPECT THAT, EVEN WHEN I STARTED NEEDING TO SHAVE EVERY DAY, I WOULD STILL BE WAY BEHIND.
HELLO?

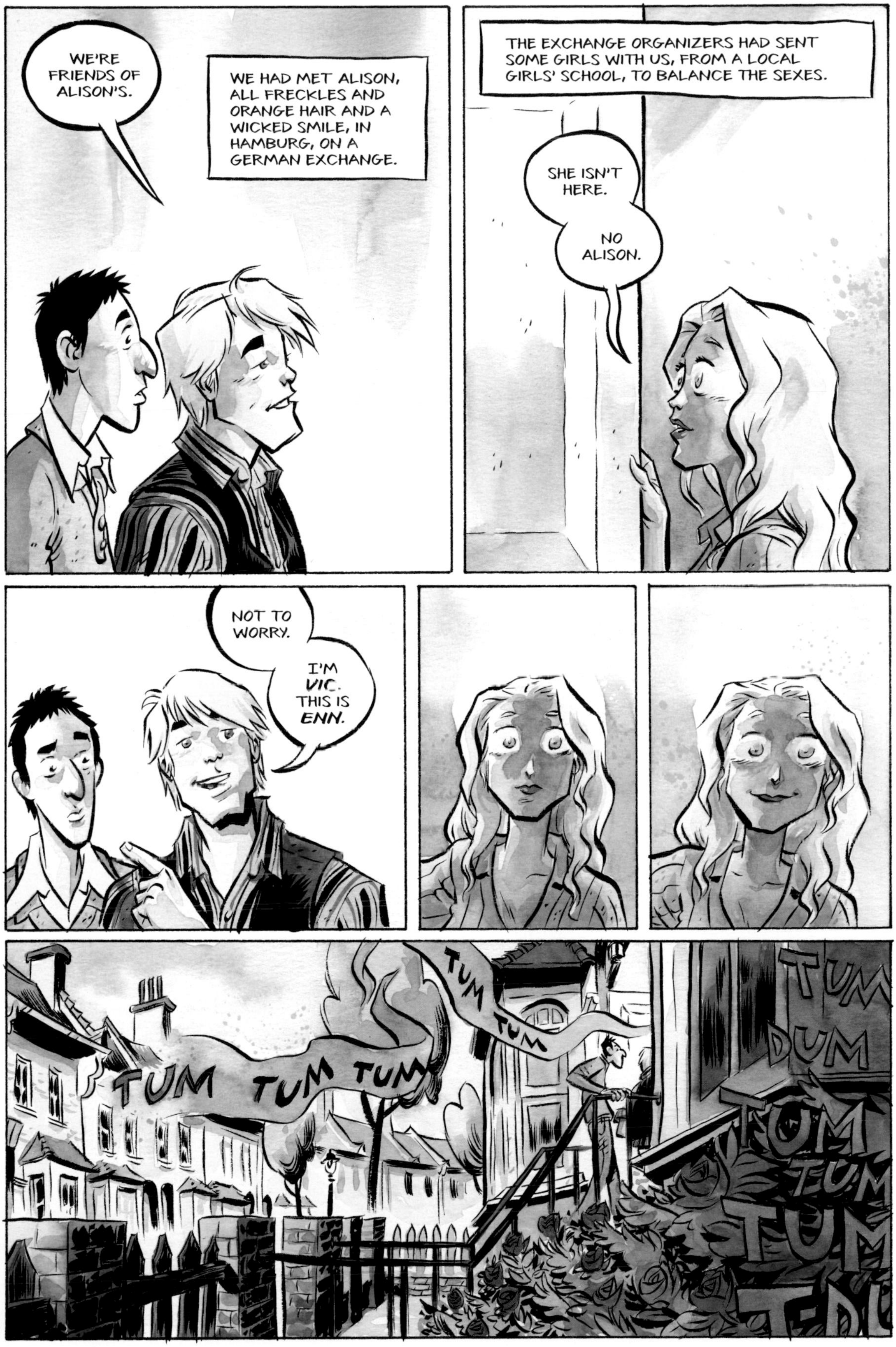
WE'RE FRIENDS OF ALISON'S.
WE HAD MET ALISON, ALL FRECKLES AND ORANGE HAIR AND A WICKED SMILE, IN HAMBURG, ON A GERMAN EXCHANGE.
THE EXCHANGE ORGANIZERS HAD SENT SOME GIRLS WITH US, FROM A LOCAL GIRLS' SCHOOL, TO BALANCE THE SEXES.
SHE ISN'T HERE.
NO ALISON.
NOT TO WORRY.
I'M *VIC*. THIS IS *ENN*.
TUM TUM TUM TUM TUM
TUM DUM TUM TUM TUM

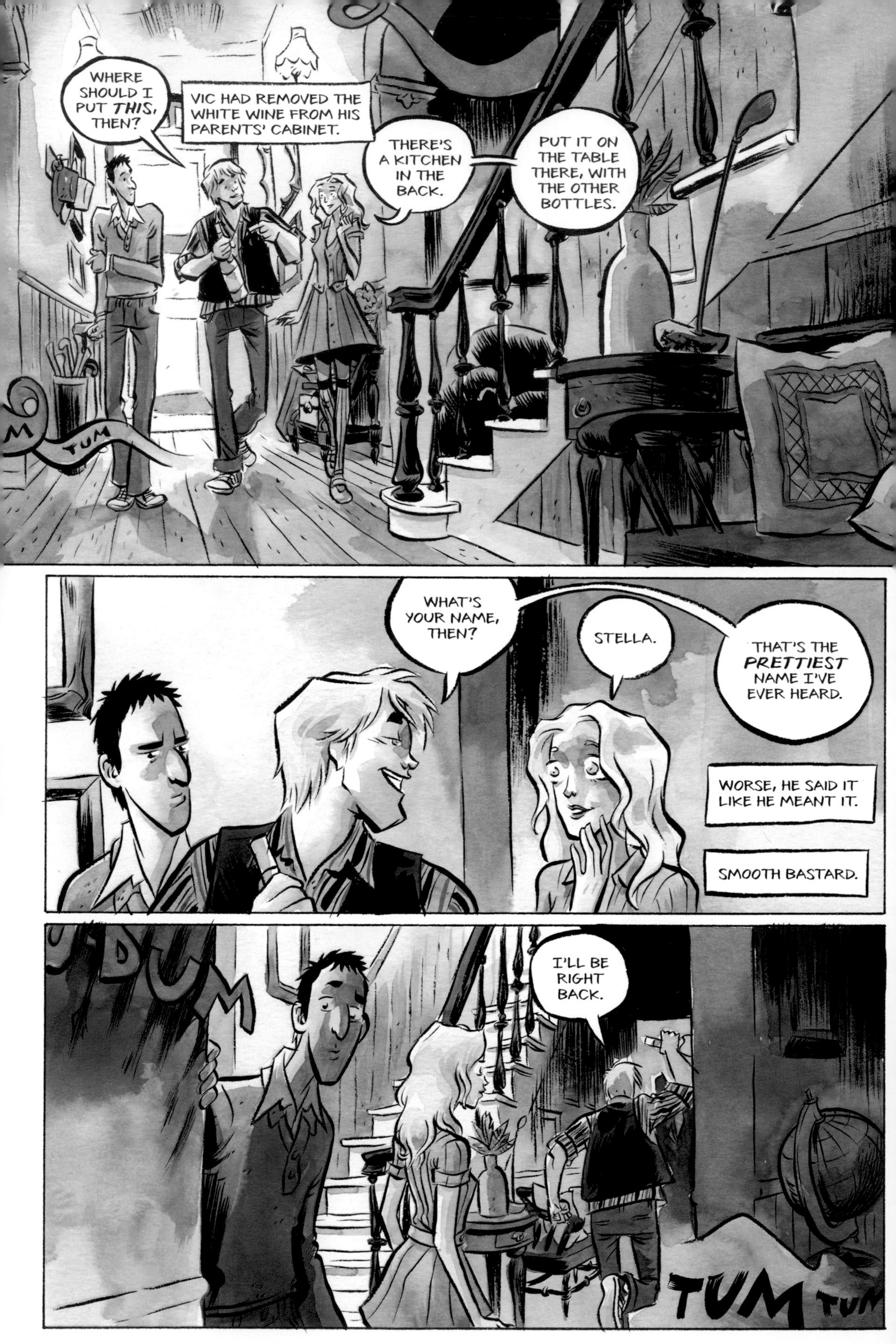
WHERE SHOULD I PUT *THIS*, THEN?
VIC HAD REMOVED THE WHITE WINE FROM HIS PARENTS' CABINET.
THERE'S A KITCHEN IN THE BACK.
PUT IT ON THE TABLE THERE, WITH THE OTHER BOTTLES.
M TUM
WHAT'S YOUR NAME, THEN?
STELLA.
THAT'S THE *PRETTIEST* NAME I'VE EVER HEARD.
WORSE, HE SAID IT LIKE HE MEANT IT.
SMOOTH BASTARD.
DUM
I'LL BE RIGHT BACK.
TUM TUM

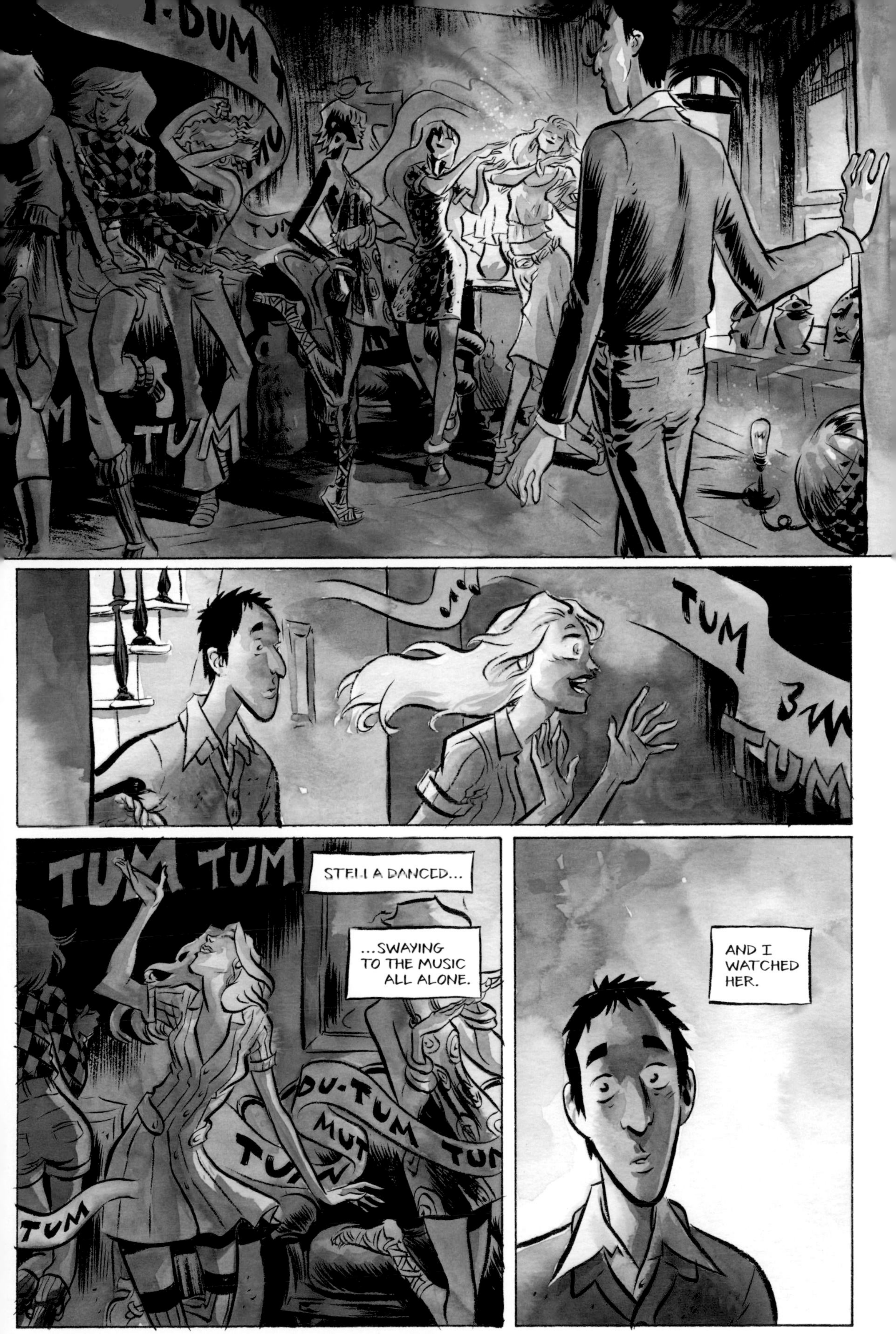
TUM
TUM
TUM
TUM TUM
STELLA DANCED...
...SWAYING TO THE MUSIC ALL ALONE.
DU-TUM
TUM
AND I WATCHED HER.

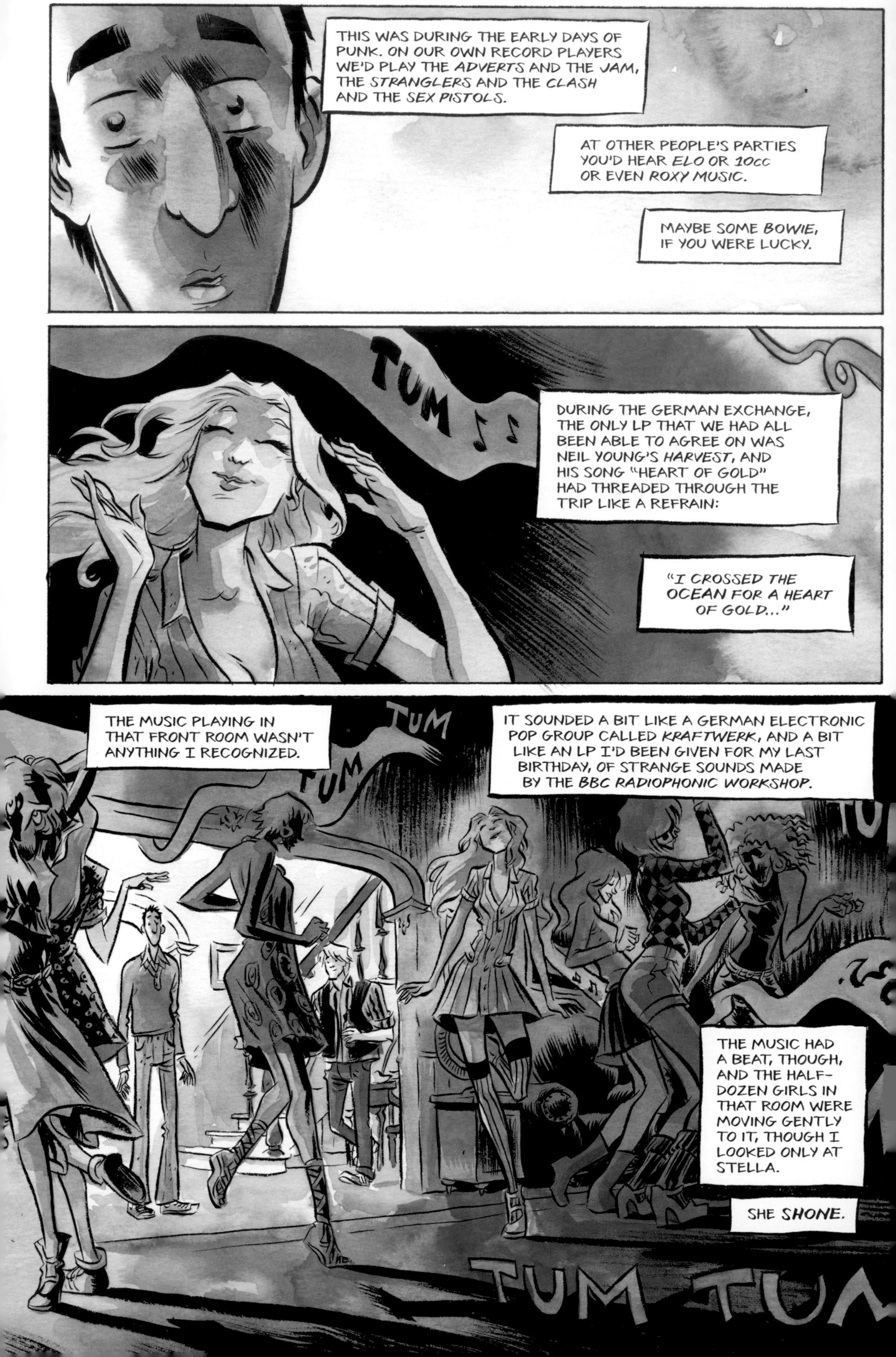
THIS WAS DURING THE EARLY DAYS OF PUNK. ON OUR OWN RECORD PLAYERS WE'D PLAY THE *ADVERTS* AND THE *JAM*, THE *STRANGLERS* AND THE *CLASH* AND THE *SEX PISTOLS*.
AT OTHER PEOPLE'S PARTIES YOU'D HEAR *ELO* OR *10cc* OR EVEN *ROXY MUSIC*.
MAYBE SOME *BOWIE*, IF YOU WERE LUCKY.
TUM
DURING THE GERMAN EXCHANGE, THE ONLY LP THAT WE HAD ALL BEEN ABLE TO AGREE ON WAS NEIL YOUNG'S *HARVEST*, AND HIS SONG "HEART OF GOLD" HAD THREADED THROUGH THE TRIP LIKE A REFRAIN:
"I CROSSED THE OCEAN FOR A HEART OF GOLD..."
THE MUSIC PLAYING IN THAT FRONT ROOM WASN'T ANYTHING I RECOGNIZED.
TUM
TUM
IT SOUNDED A BIT LIKE A GERMAN ELECTRONIC POP GROUP CALLED *KRAFTWERK*, AND A BIT LIKE AN LP I'D BEEN GIVEN FOR MY LAST BIRTHDAY, OF STRANGE SOUNDS MADE BY THE *BBC RADIOPHONIC WORKSHOP*.
THE MUSIC HAD A BEAT, THOUGH, AND THE HALF-DOZEN GIRLS IN THAT ROOM WERE MOVING GENTLY TO IT, THOUGH I LOOKED ONLY AT STELLA.
SHE *SHONE*.
TUM TUM

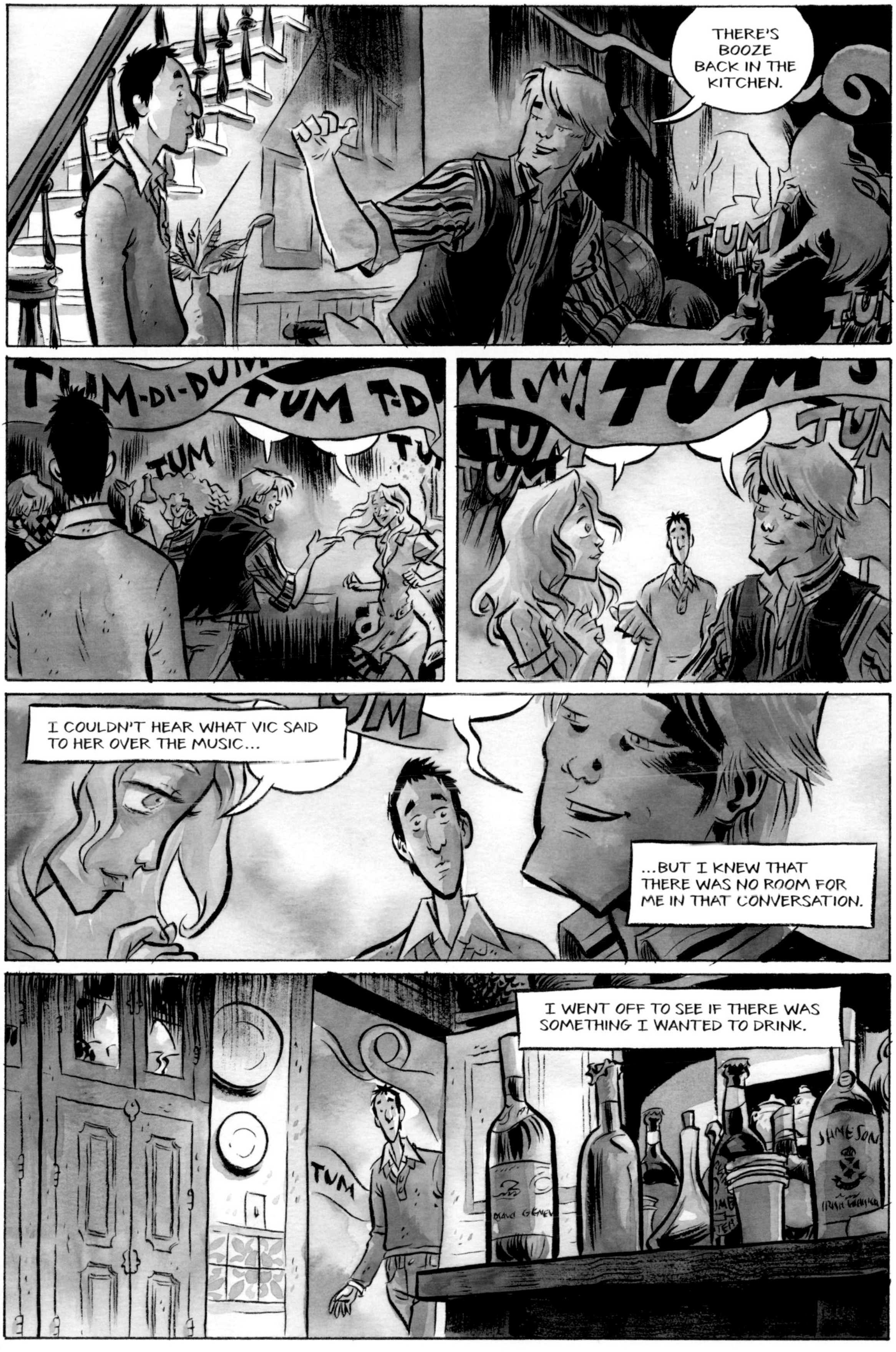
THERE'S BOOZE BACK IN THE KITCHEN.
TUM
TUM
TUM-DI-DUM TUM T-D
TUM
TUM
TUM
TUM
TUM
I COULDN'T HEAR WHAT VIC SAID TO HER OVER THE MUSIC...
...BUT I KNEW THAT THERE WAS NO ROOM FOR ME IN THAT CONVERSATION.
I WENT OFF TO SEE IF THERE WAS SOMETHING I WANTED TO DRINK.
TUM

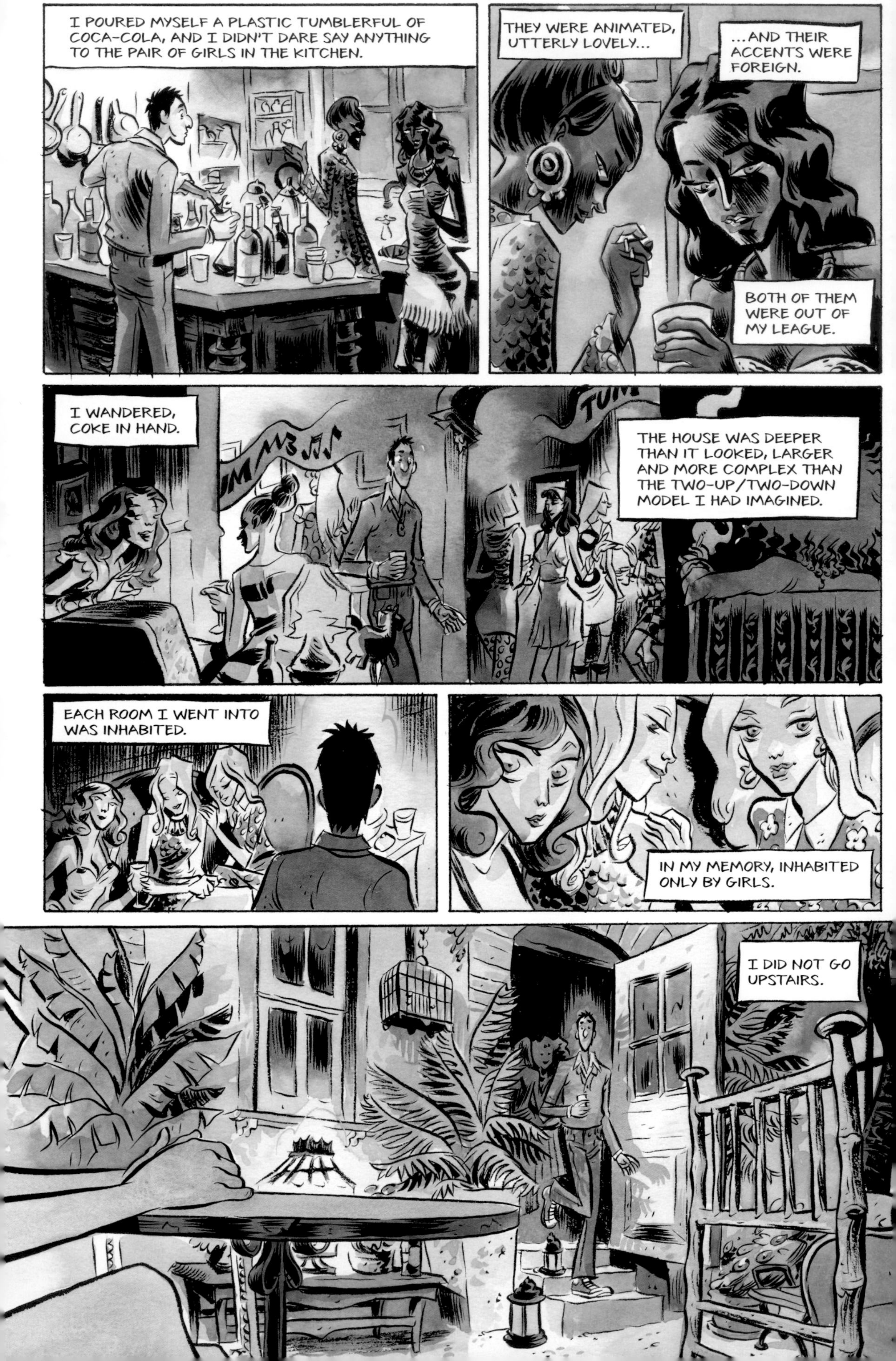
I POURED MYSELF A PLASTIC TUMBLERFUL OF COCA-COLA, AND I DIDN'T DARE SAY ANYTHING TO THE PAIR OF GIRLS IN THE KITCHEN.
THEY WERE ANIMATED, UTTERLY LOVELY...
...AND THEIR ACCENTS WERE FOREIGN.
BOTH OF THEM WERE OUT OF MY LEAGUE.
I WANDERED, COKE IN HAND.
THE HOUSE WAS DEEPER THAN IT LOOKED, LARGER AND MORE COMPLEX THAN THE TWO-UP/TWO-DOWN MODEL I HAD IMAGINED.
EACH ROOM I WENT INTO WAS INHABITED.
IN MY MEMORY, INHABITED ONLY BY GIRLS.
I DID NOT GO UPSTAIRS.

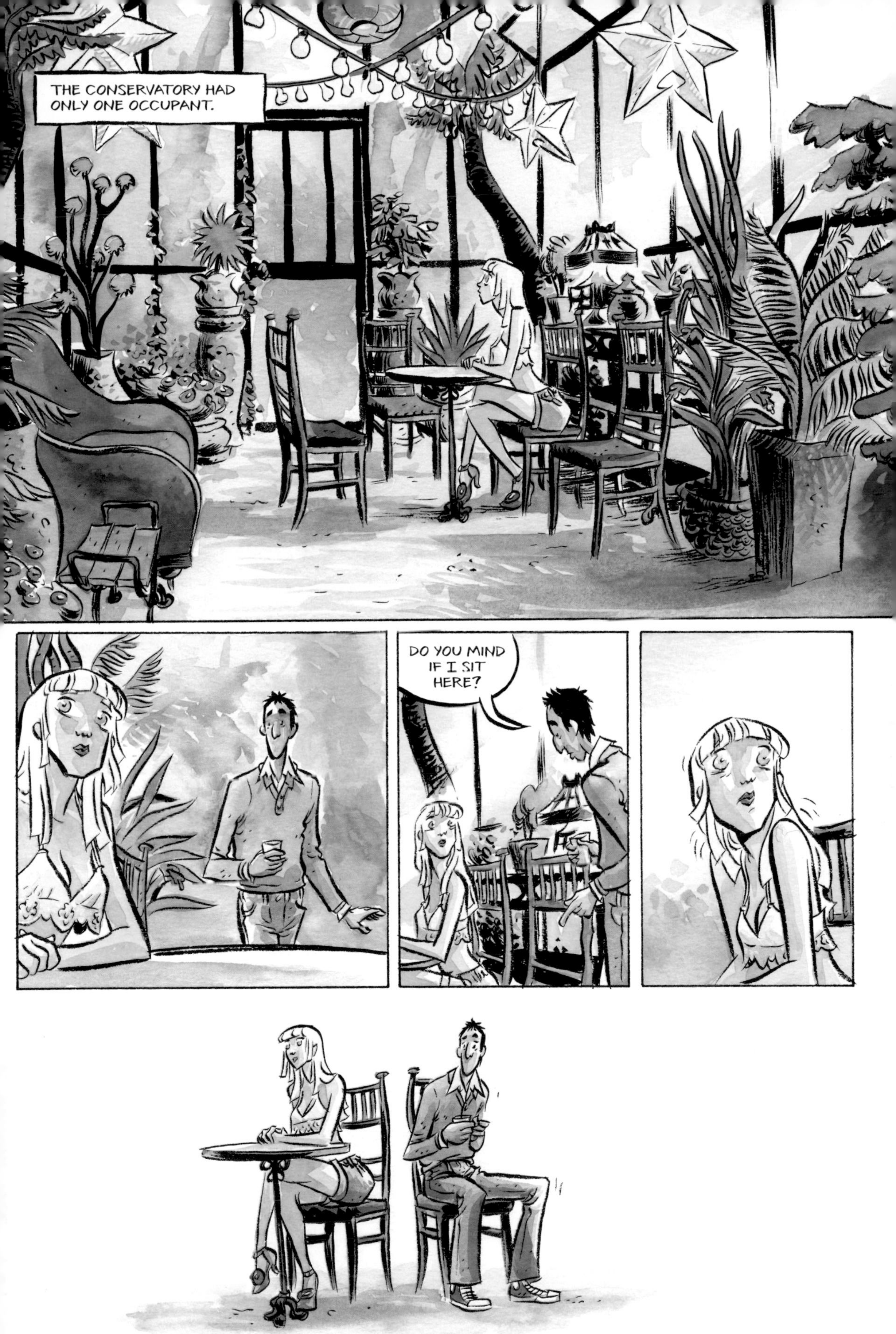
THE CONSERVATORY HAD ONLY ONE OCCUPANT.
DO YOU MIND IF I SIT HERE?

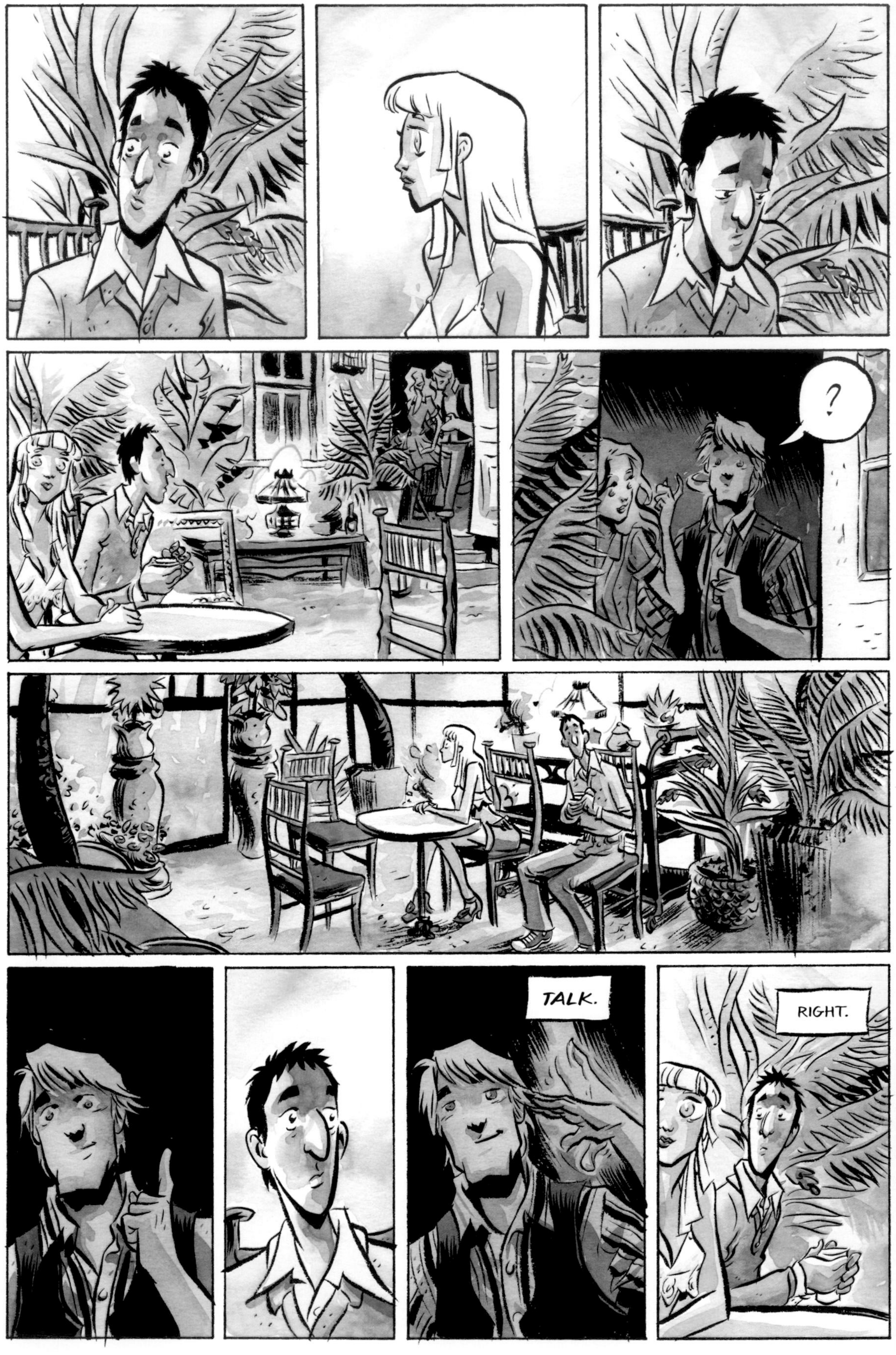
?
TALK.
RIGHT.

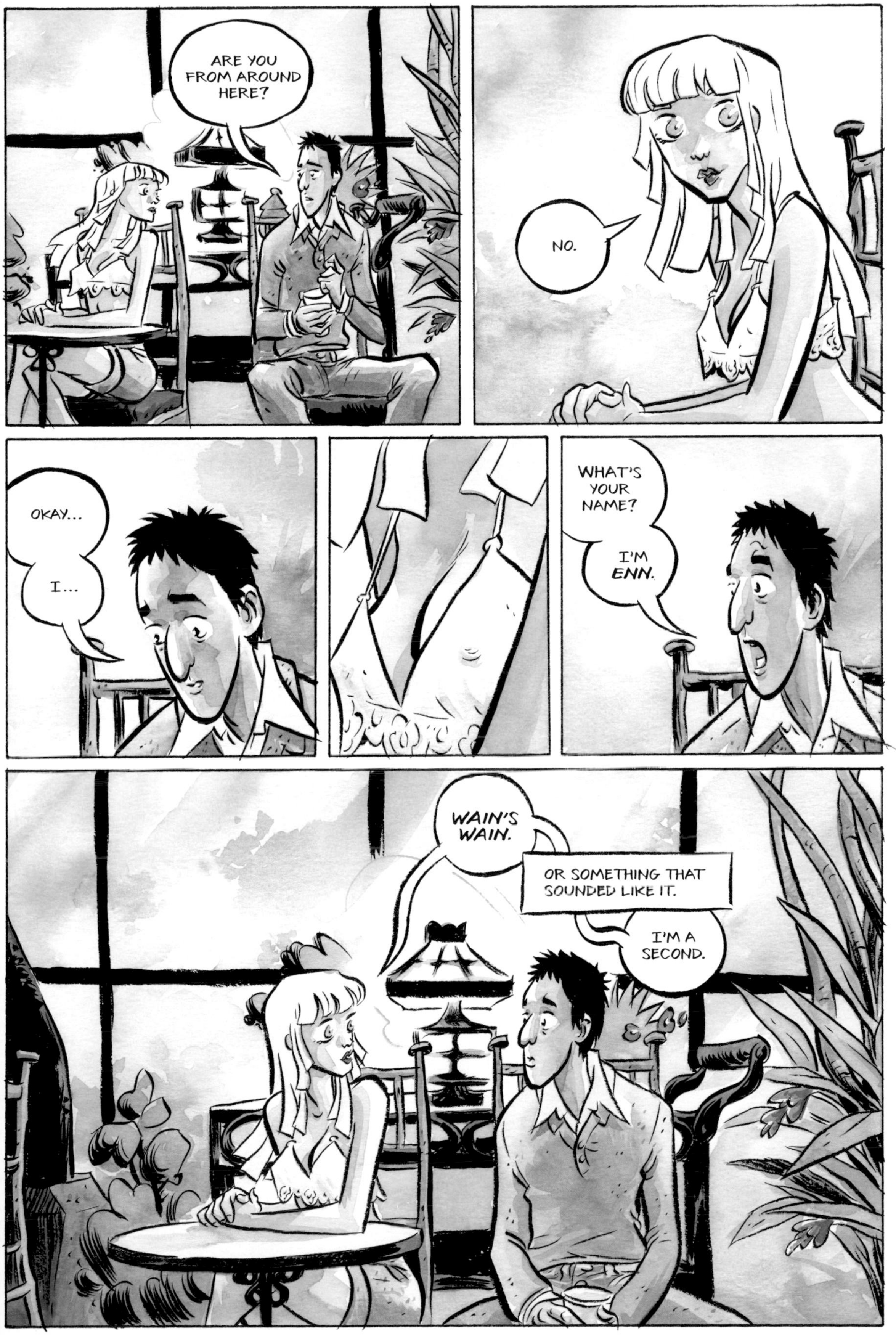
ARE YOU FROM AROUND HERE?
NO.
OKAY...
I...
WHAT'S YOUR NAME?
I'M ENN.
WAIN'S WAIN.
OR SOMETHING THAT SOUNDED LIKE IT.
I'M A SECOND.

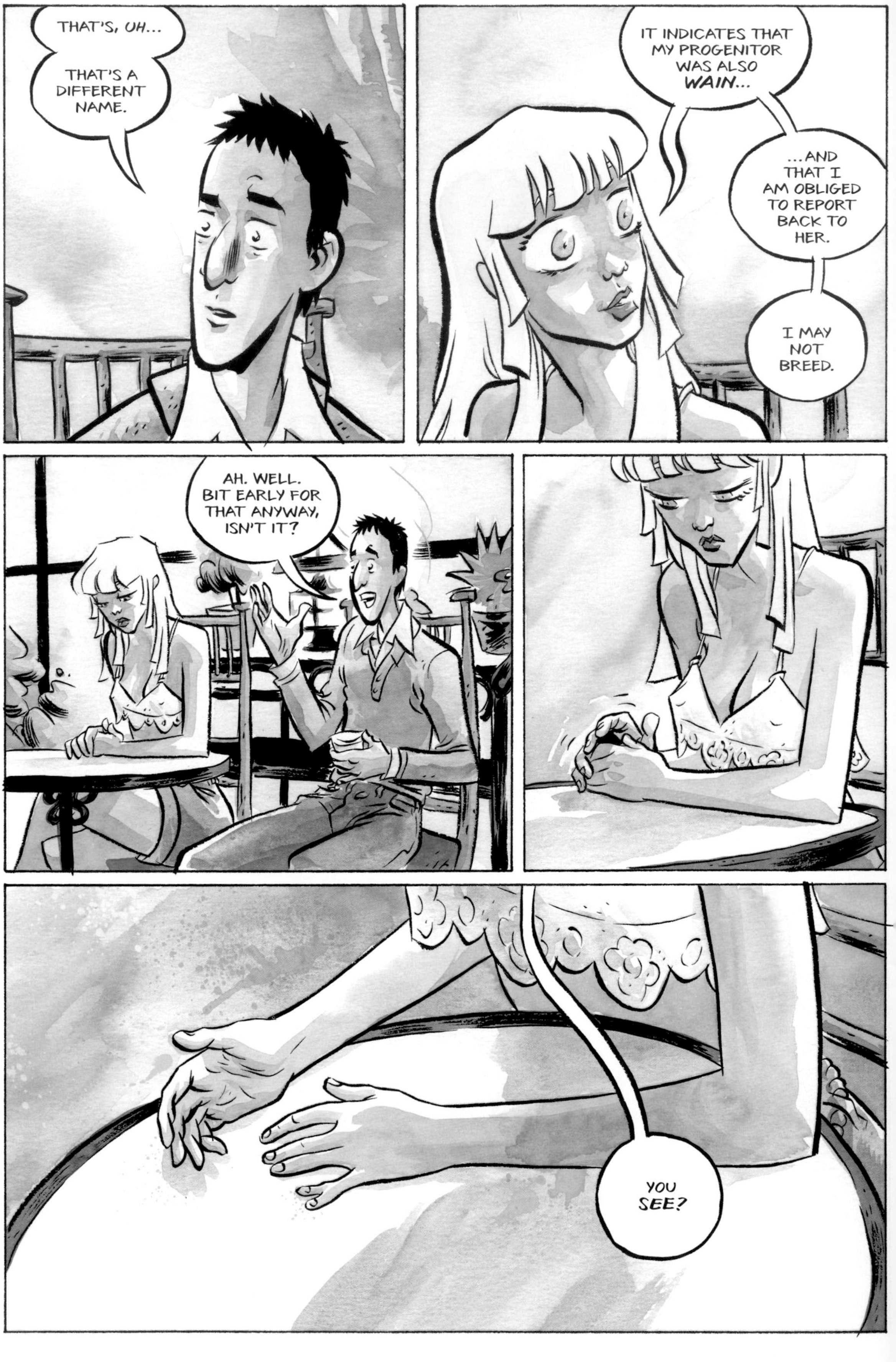
THAT'S, UH...
THAT'S A DIFFERENT NAME.
IT INDICATES THAT MY PROGENITOR WAS ALSO WAIN...
...AND THAT I AM OBLIGED TO REPORT BACK TO HER.
I MAY NOT BREED.
AH. WELL. BIT EARLY FOR THAT ANYWAY, ISN'T IT?
YOU SEE?

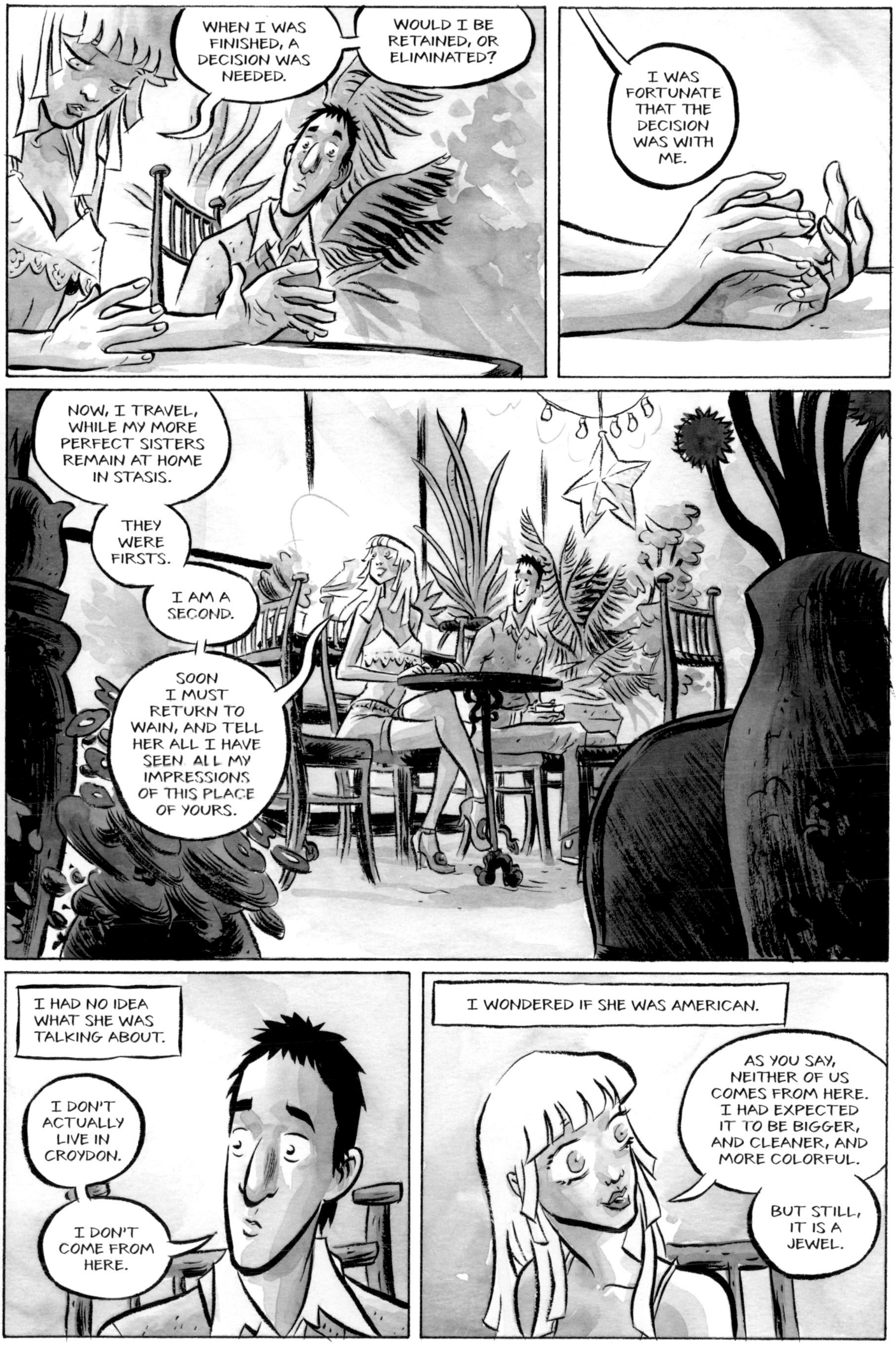
WHEN I WAS FINISHED, A DECISION WAS NEEDED.
WOULD I BE RETAINED, OR ELIMINATED?
I WAS FORTUNATE THAT THE DECISION WAS WITH ME.
NOW, I TRAVEL, WHILE MY MORE PERFECT SISTERS REMAIN AT HOME IN STASIS.
THEY WERE FIRSTS.
I AM A SECOND.
SOON I MUST RETURN TO WAIN, AND TELL HER ALL I HAVE SEEN. ALL MY IMPRESSIONS OF THIS PLACE OF YOURS.
I HAD NO IDEA WHAT SHE WAS TALKING ABOUT.
I DON'T ACTUALLY LIVE IN CROYDON.
I DON'T COME FROM HERE.
I WONDERED IF SHE WAS AMERICAN.
AS YOU SAY, NEITHER OF US COMES FROM HERE. I HAD EXPECTED IT TO BE BIGGER, AND CLEANER, AND MORE COLORFUL.
BUT STILL, IT IS A JEWEL.

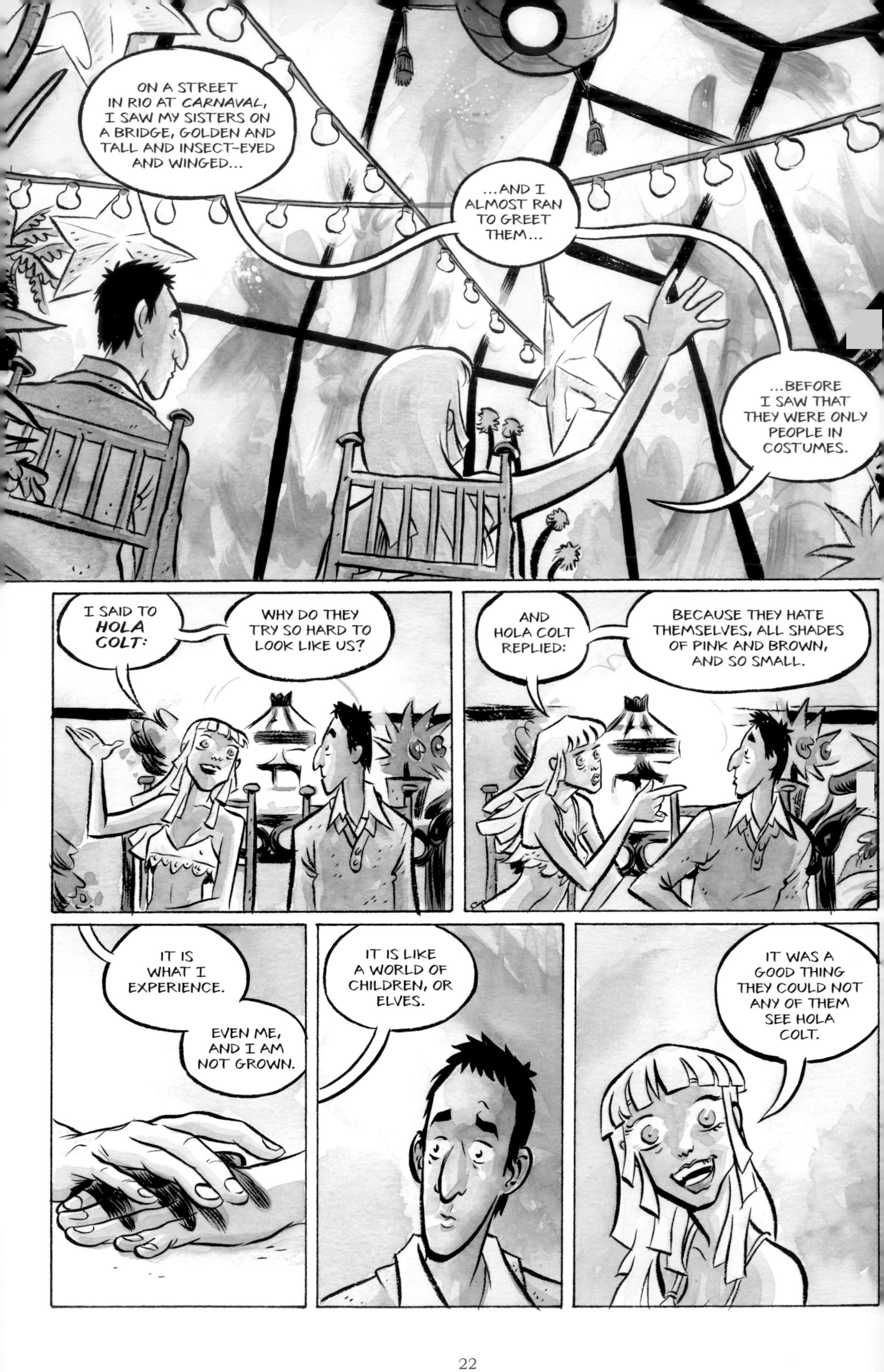

ON A STREET IN RIO AT CARNAVAL, I SAW MY SISTERS ON A BRIDGE, GOLDEN AND TALL AND INSECT-EYED AND WINGED...
...AND I ALMOST RAN TO GREET THEM...
...BEFORE I SAW THAT THEY WERE ONLY PEOPLE IN COSTUMES.
I SAID TO HOLA COLT:
WHY DO THEY TRY SO HARD TO LOOK LIKE US?
AND HOLA COLT REPLIED:
BECAUSE THEY HATE THEMSELVES, ALL SHADES OF PINK AND BROWN, AND SO SMALL.
IT IS WHAT I EXPERIENCE.
EVEN ME, AND I AM NOT GROWN.
IT IS LIKE A WORLD OF CHILDREN, OR ELVES.
IT WAS A GOOD THING THEY COULD NOT ANY OF THEM SEE HOLA COLT.

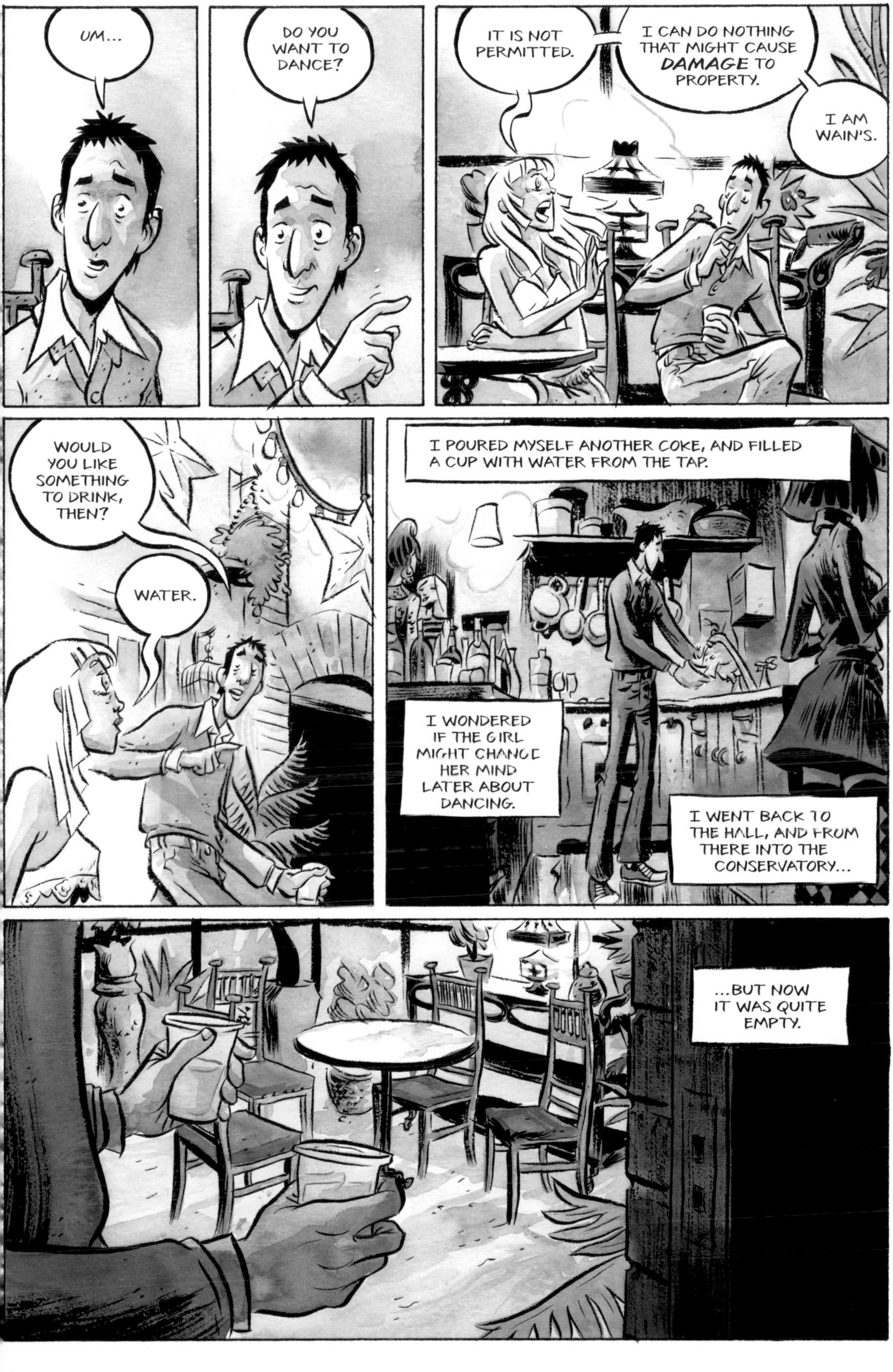
UM...
DO YOU WANT TO DANCE?
IT IS NOT PERMITTED.
I CAN DO NOTHING THAT MIGHT CAUSE DAMAGE TO PROPERTY.
I AM WAIN'S.
WOULD YOU LIKE SOMETHING TO DRINK, THEN?
WATER.
I POURED MYSELF ANOTHER COKE, AND FILLED A CUP WITH WATER FROM THE TAP.
I WONDERED IF THE GIRL MIGHT CHANGE HER MIND LATER ABOUT DANCING.
I WENT BACK TO THE HALL, AND FROM THERE INTO THE CONSERVATORY...
...BUT NOW IT WAS QUITE EMPTY.

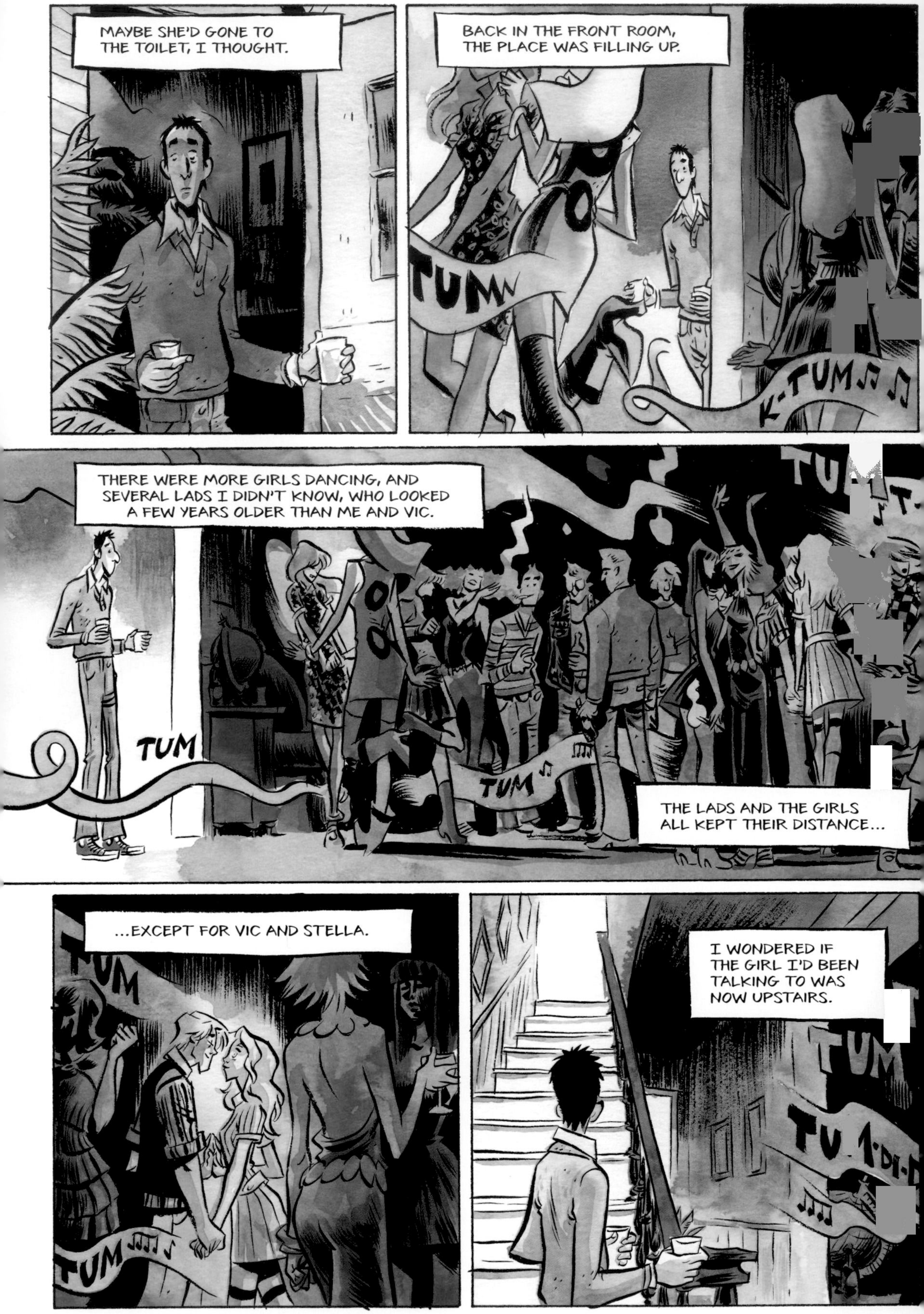
MAYBE SHE'D GONE TO THE TOILET, I THOUGHT.
BACK IN THE FRONT ROOM, THE PLACE WAS FILLING UP.
TUM
K-TUM
THERE WERE MORE GIRLS DANCING, AND SEVERAL LADS I DIDN'T KNOW, WHO LOOKED A FEW YEARS OLDER THAN ME AND VIC.
TUM
TUM
TUM
THE LADS AND THE GIRLS ALL KEPT THEIR DISTANCE...
...EXCEPT FOR VIC AND STELLA.
TUM
TUM
I WONDERED IF THE GIRL I'D BEEN TALKING TO WAS NOW UPSTAIRS.
TUM
TU 1-DI-

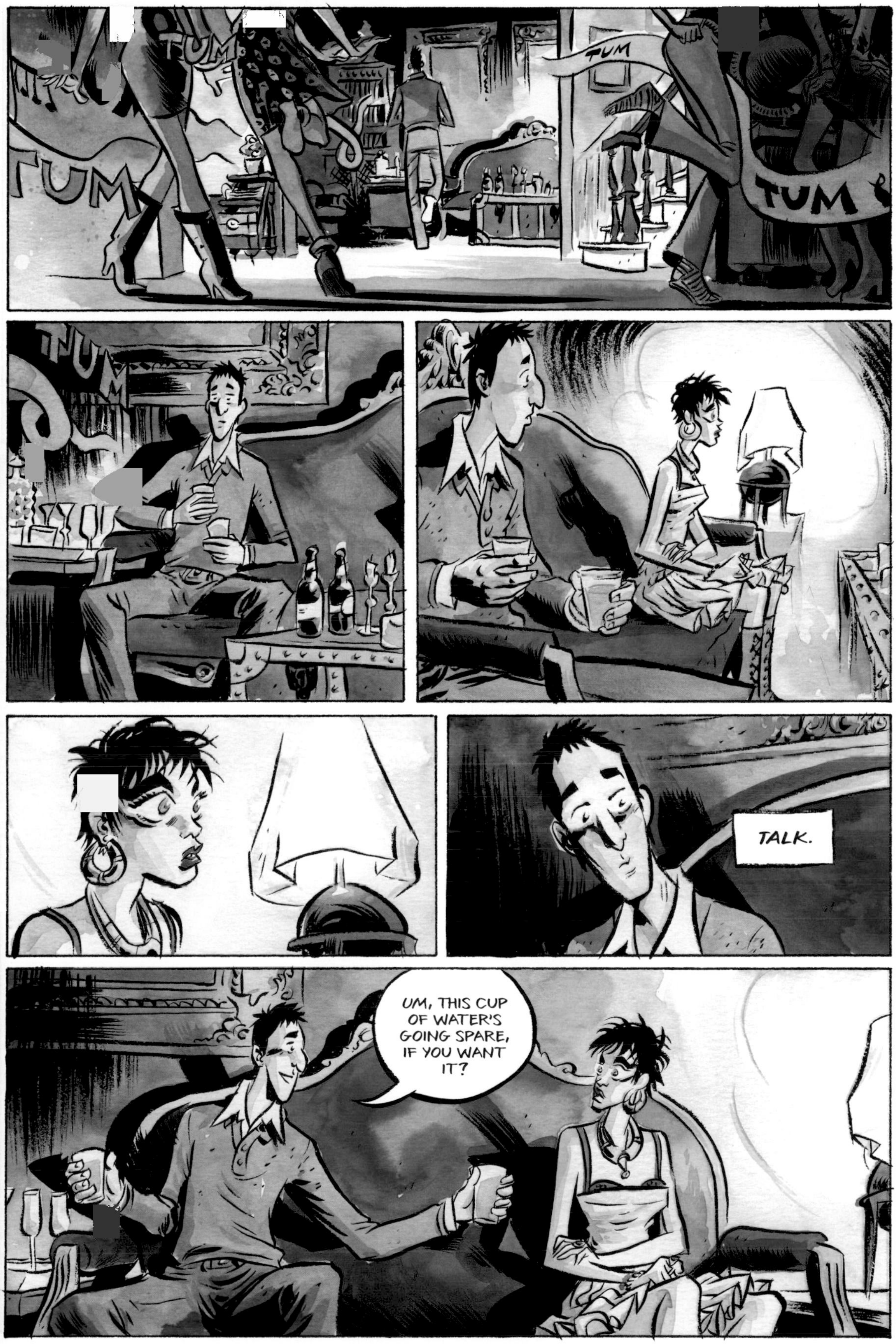
TUM
TUM
TUM
TUM
TUM
TALK.
UM, THIS CUP OF WATER'S GOING SPARE, IF YOU WANT IT?

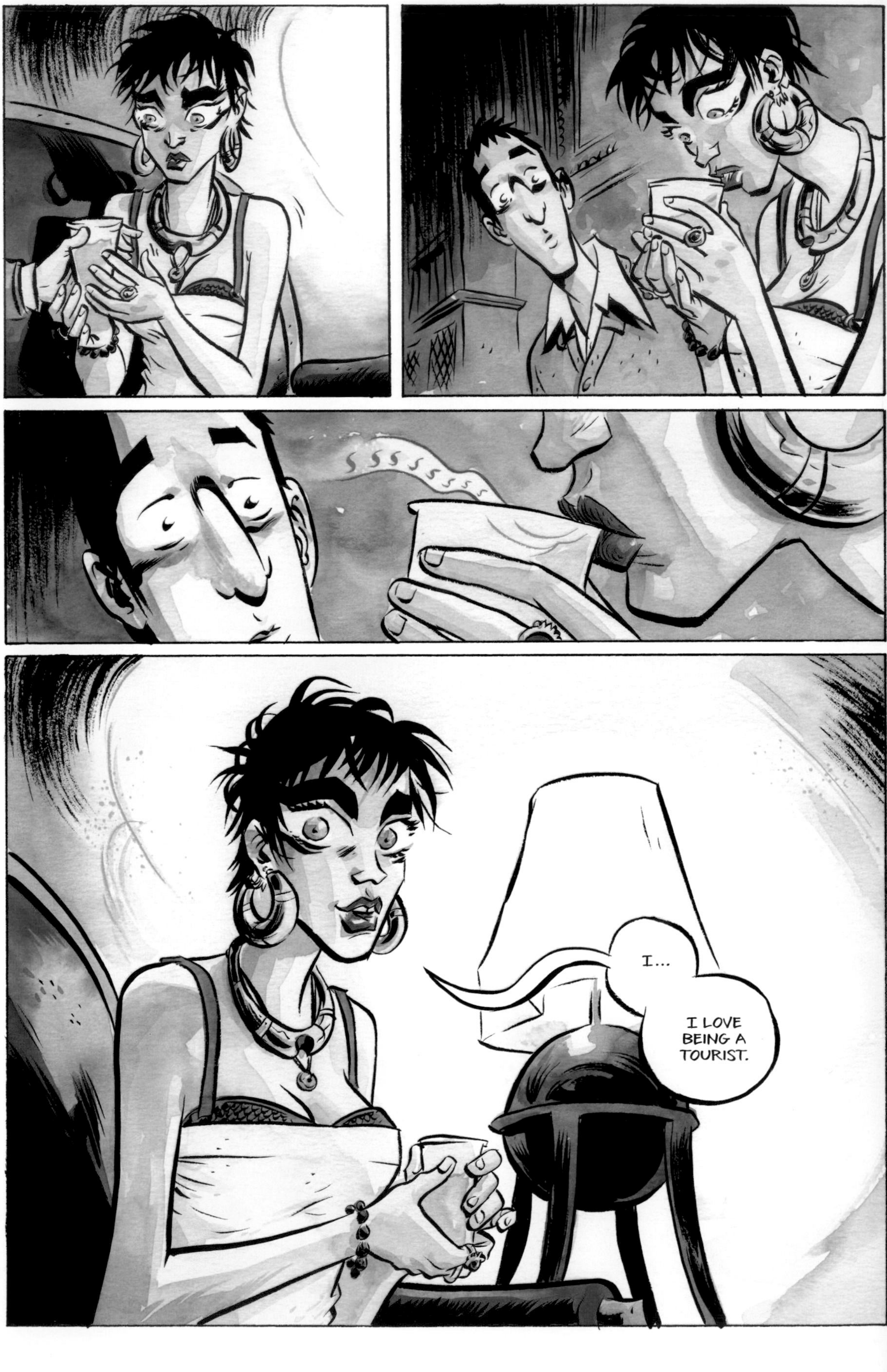
SSSSSSSSS
I...
I LOVE BEING A TOURIST.

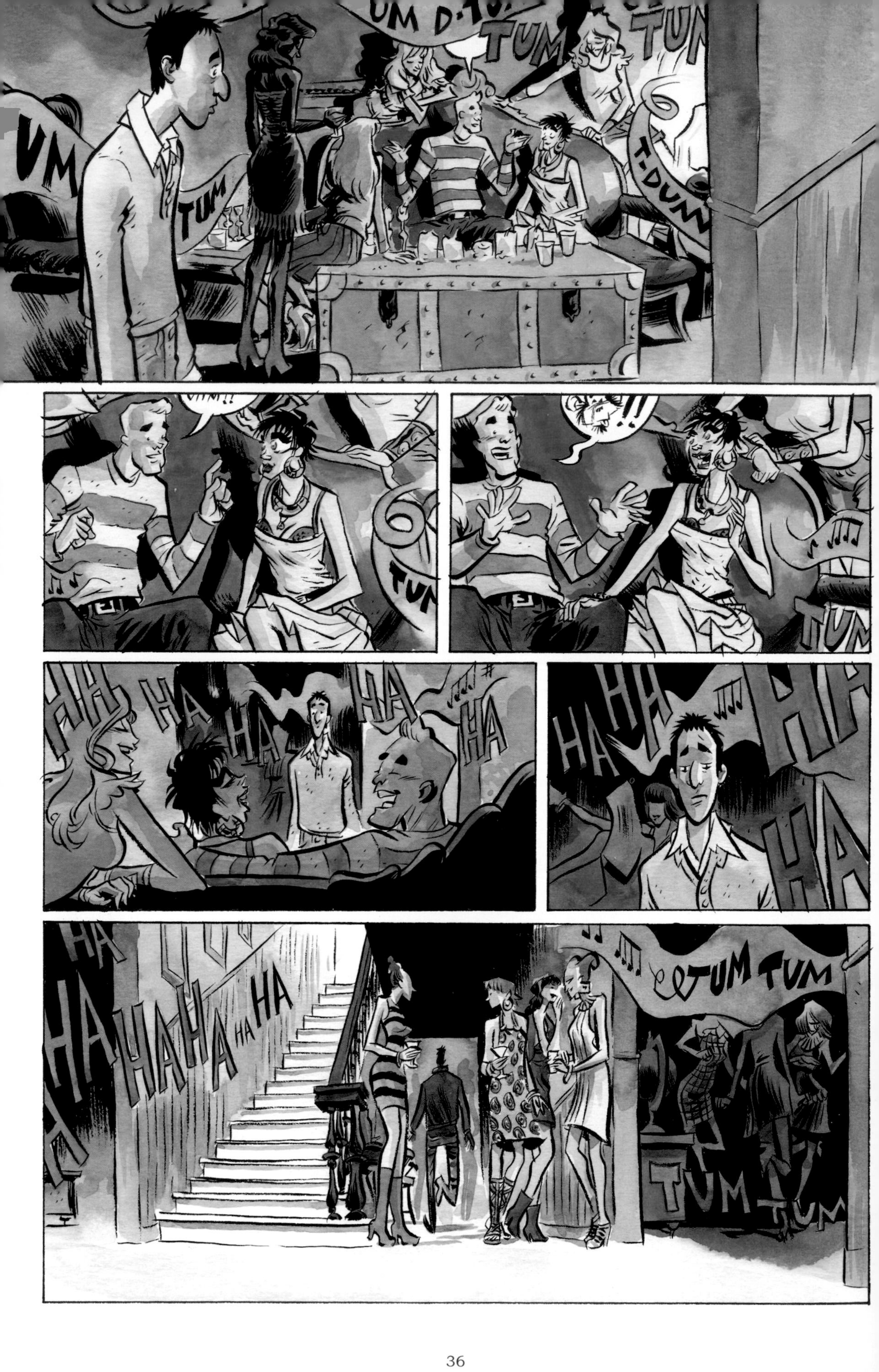
TUM
TUM
UM
TUM
T-DUM
TUM
TUM
HA HA HA HA HA HA
HA HA HA HA
HA HAHAHA HA HA
TUM TUM
TUM TUM

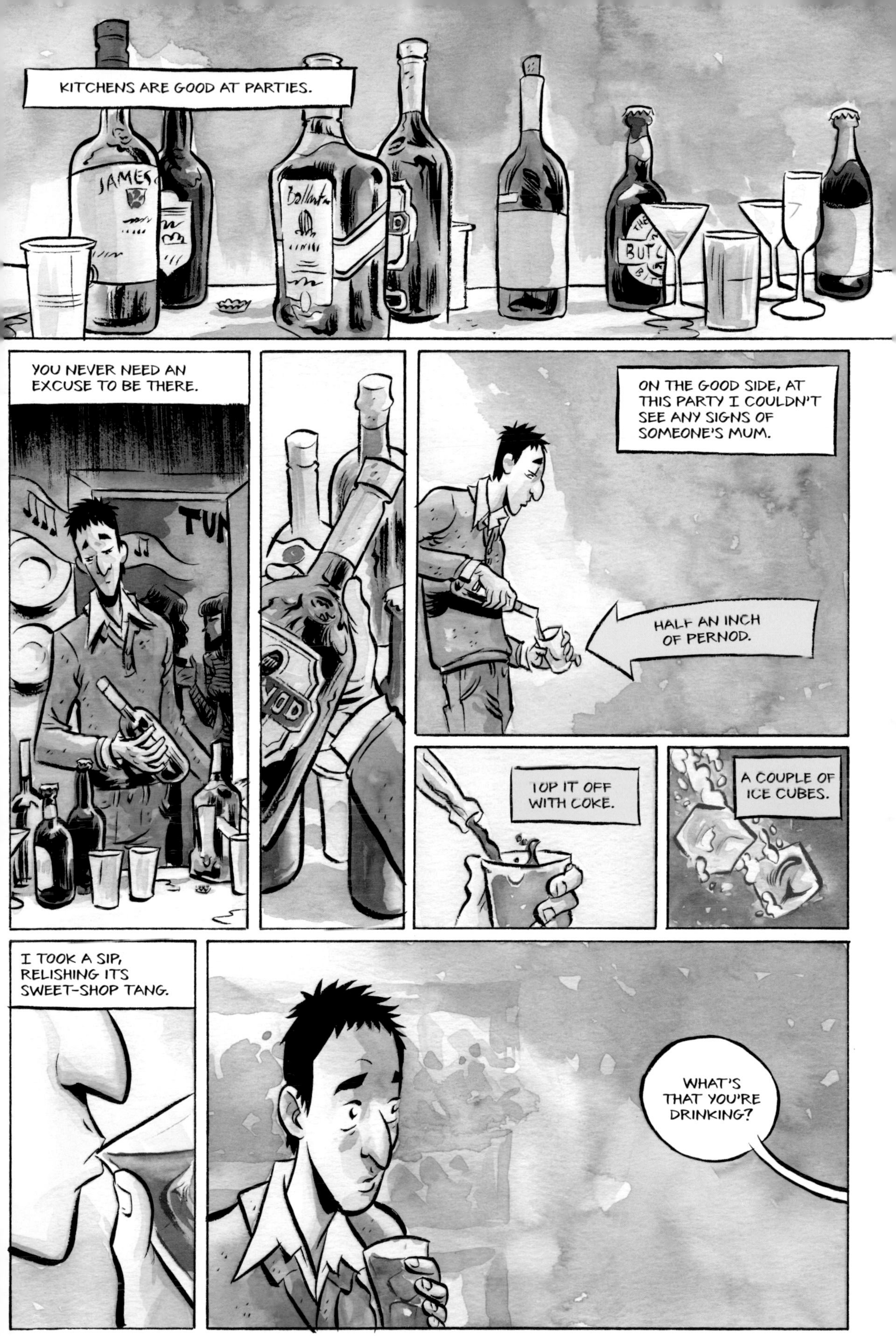
KITCHENS ARE GOOD AT PARTIES.
YOU NEVER NEED AN EXCUSE TO BE THERE.
ON THE GOOD SIDE, AT THIS PARTY I COULDN'T SEE ANY SIGNS OF SOMEONE'S MUM.
HALF AN INCH OF PERNOD.
TOP IT OFF WITH COKE.
A COUPLE OF ICE CUBES.
I TOOK A SIP, RELISHING ITS SWEET-SHOP TANG.
WHAT'S THAT YOU'RE DRINKING?

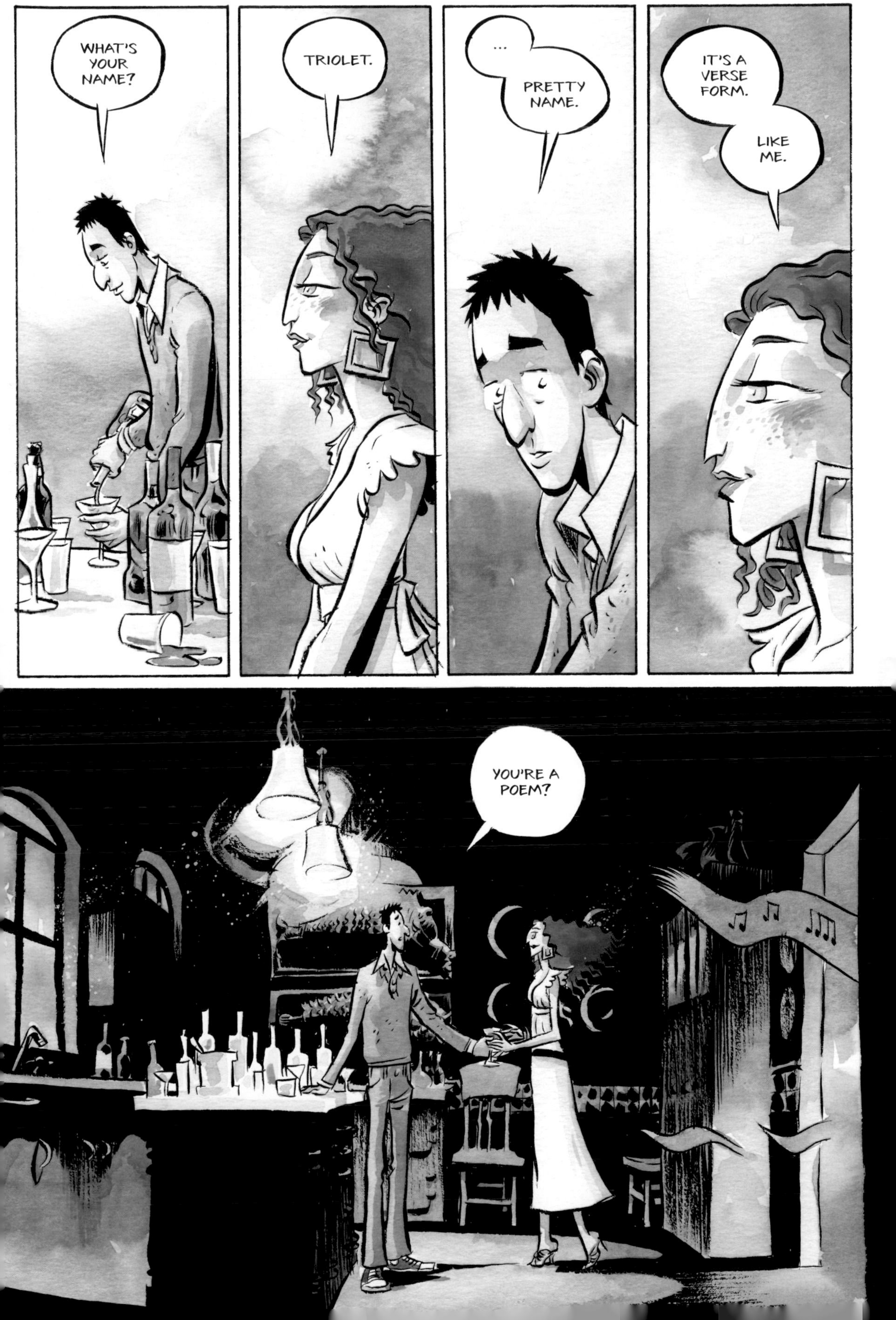
WHAT'S YOUR NAME?
TRIOLET.
...
PRETTY NAME.
IT'S A VERSE FORM.
LIKE ME.
YOU'RE A POEM?

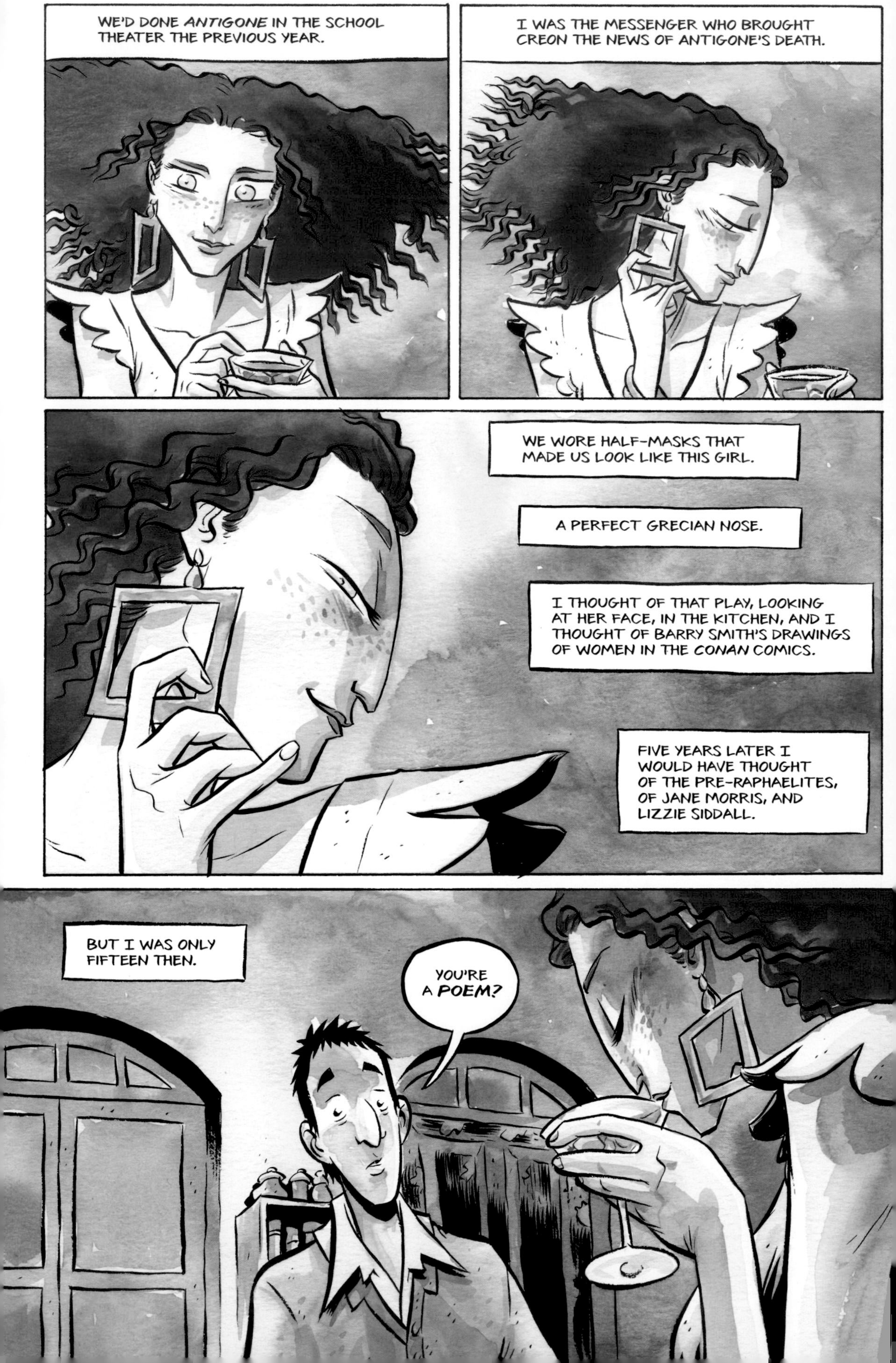
WE'D DONE *ANTIGONE* IN THE SCHOOL THEATER THE PREVIOUS YEAR.
I WAS THE MESSENGER WHO BROUGHT CREON THE NEWS OF ANTIGONE'S DEATH.
WE WORE HALF-MASKS THAT MADE US LOOK LIKE THIS GIRL.
A PERFECT GRECIAN NOSE.
I THOUGHT OF THAT PLAY, LOOKING AT HER FACE, IN THE KITCHEN, AND I THOUGHT OF BARRY SMITH'S DRAWINGS OF WOMEN IN THE *CONAN* COMICS.
FIVE YEARS LATER I WOULD HAVE THOUGHT OF THE PRE-RAPHAELITES, OF JANE MORRIS, AND LIZZIE SIDDALL.
BUT I WAS ONLY FIFTEEN THEN.
YOU'RE A **POEM?**

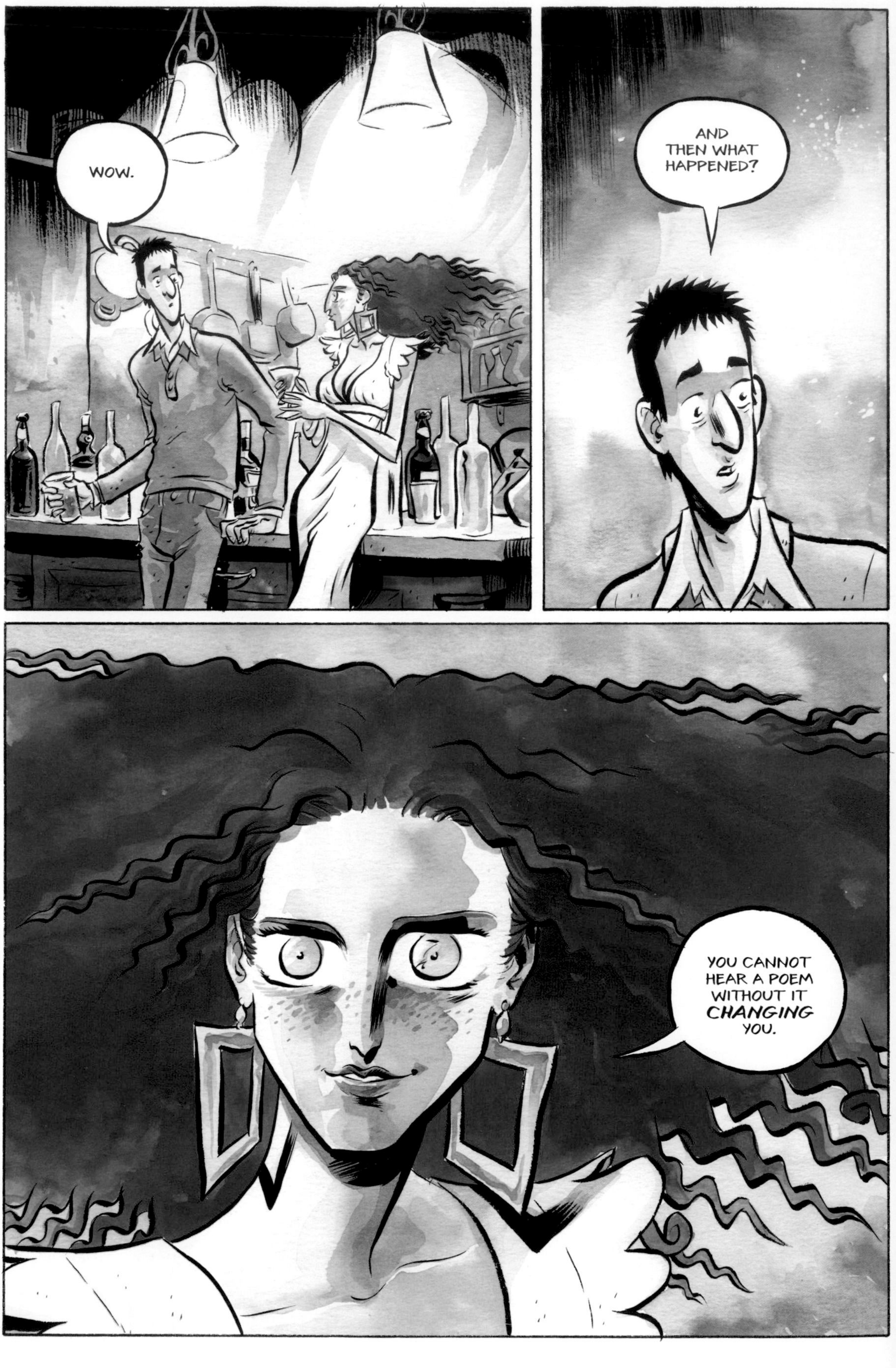
WOW.
AND THEN WHAT HAPPENED?
YOU CANNOT HEAR A POEM WITHOUT IT CHANGING YOU.

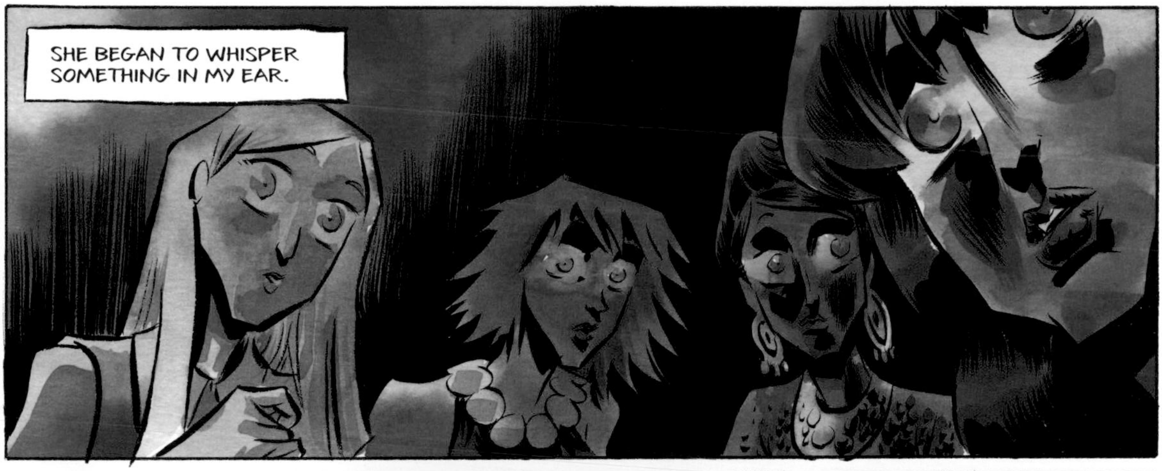
SHE BEGAN TO WHISPER SOMETHING IN MY EAR.

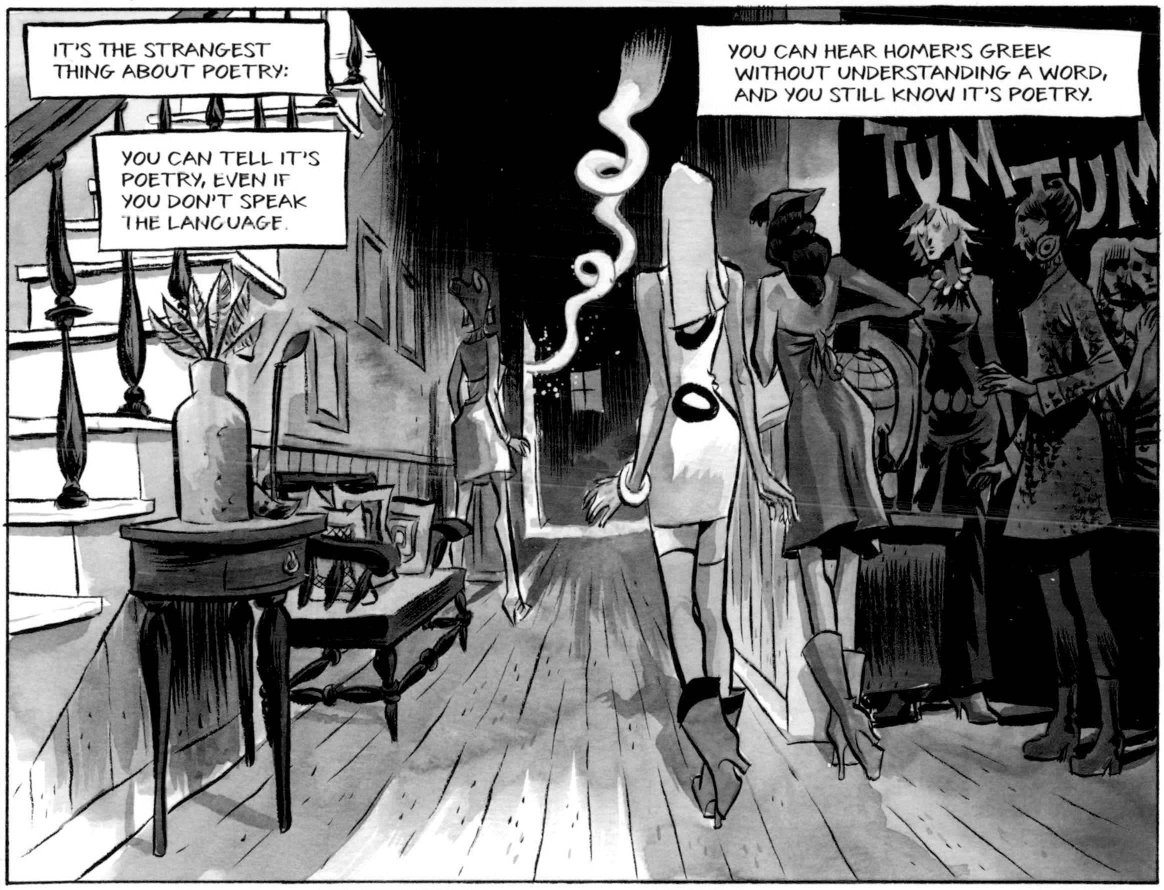
IT'S THE STRANGEST THING ABOUT POETRY:
YOU CAN TELL IT'S POETRY, EVEN IF YOU DON'T SPEAK THE LANGUAGE.
YOU CAN HEAR HOMER'S GREEK WITHOUT UNDERSTANDING A WORD, AND YOU STILL KNOW IT'S POETRY.
TUM TUM

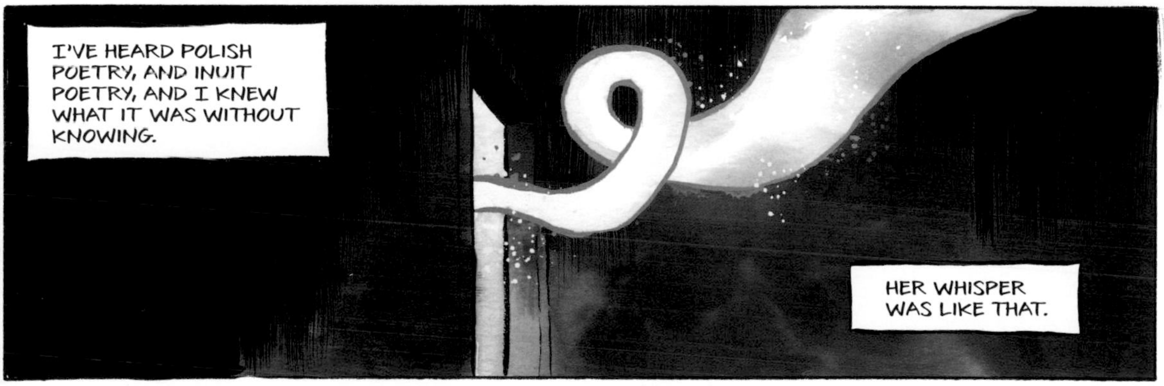
I'VE HEARD POLISH POETRY, AND INUIT POETRY, AND I KNEW WHAT IT WAS WITHOUT KNOWING.
HER WHISPER WAS LIKE THAT.

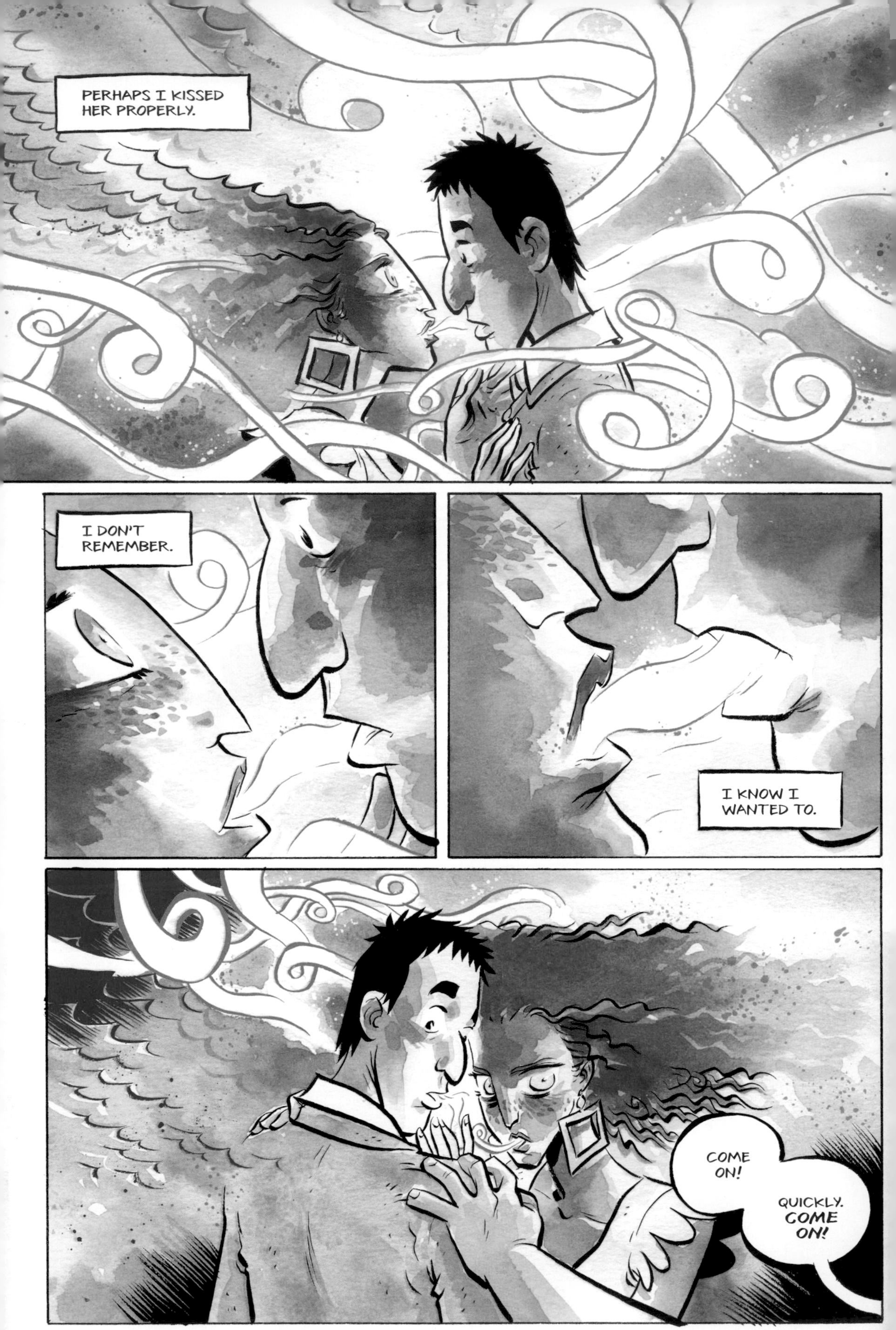
PERHAPS I KISSED HER PROPERLY.
I DON'T REMEMBER.
I KNOW I WANTED TO.
COME ON!
QUICKLY. COME ON!

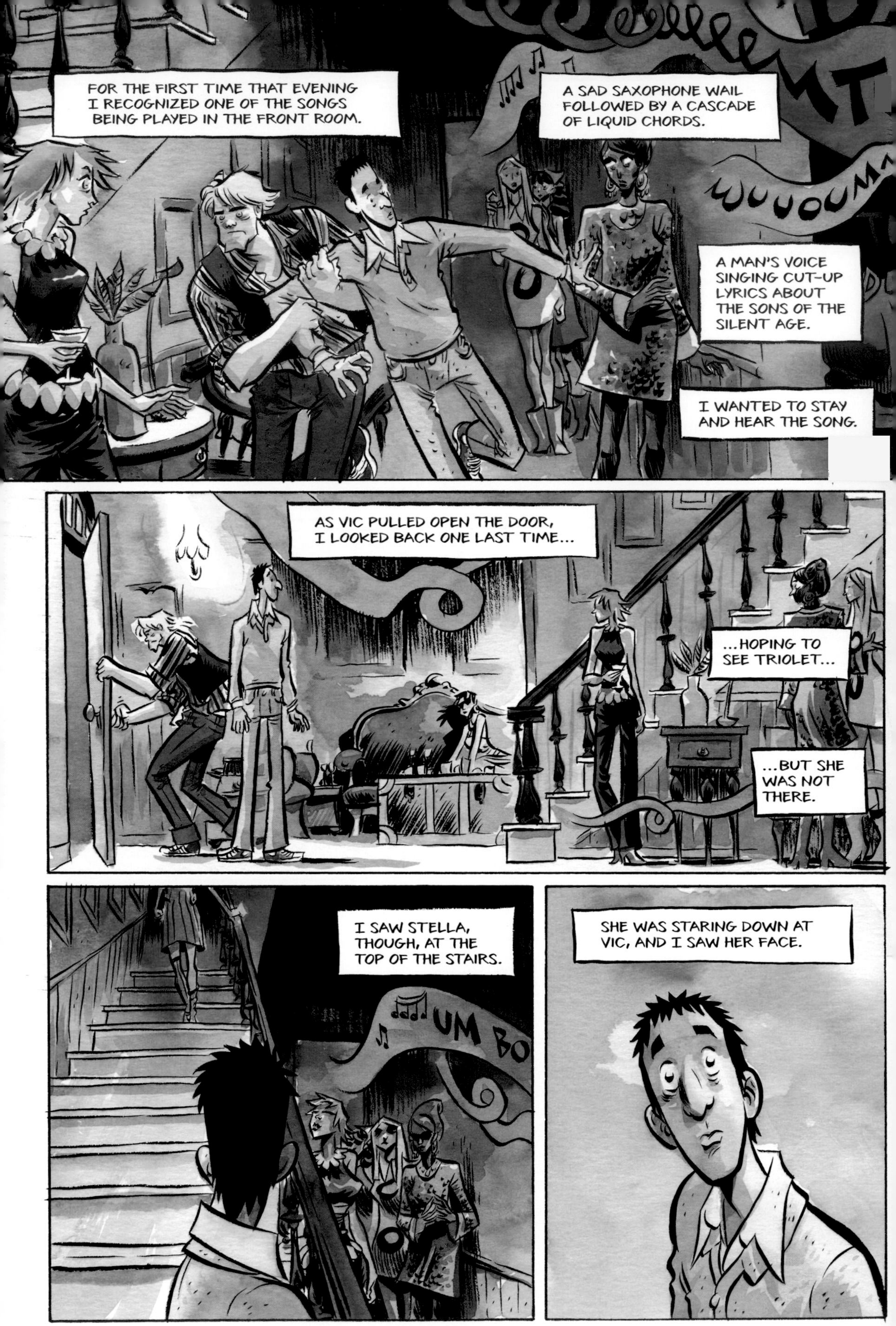
FOR THE FIRST TIME THAT EVENING I RECOGNIZED ONE OF THE SONGS BEING PLAYED IN THE FRONT ROOM.
A SAD SAXOPHONE WAIL FOLLOWED BY A CASCADE OF LIQUID CHORDS.
A MAN'S VOICE SINGING CUT-UP LYRICS ABOUT THE SONS OF THE SILENT AGE.
I WANTED TO STAY AND HEAR THE SONG.
AS VIC PULLED OPEN THE DOOR, I LOOKED BACK ONE LAST TIME...
...HOPING TO SEE TRIOLET...
...BUT SHE WAS NOT THERE.
I SAW STELLA, THOUGH, AT THE TOP OF THE STAIRS.
SHE WAS STARING DOWN AT VIC, AND I SAW HER FACE.

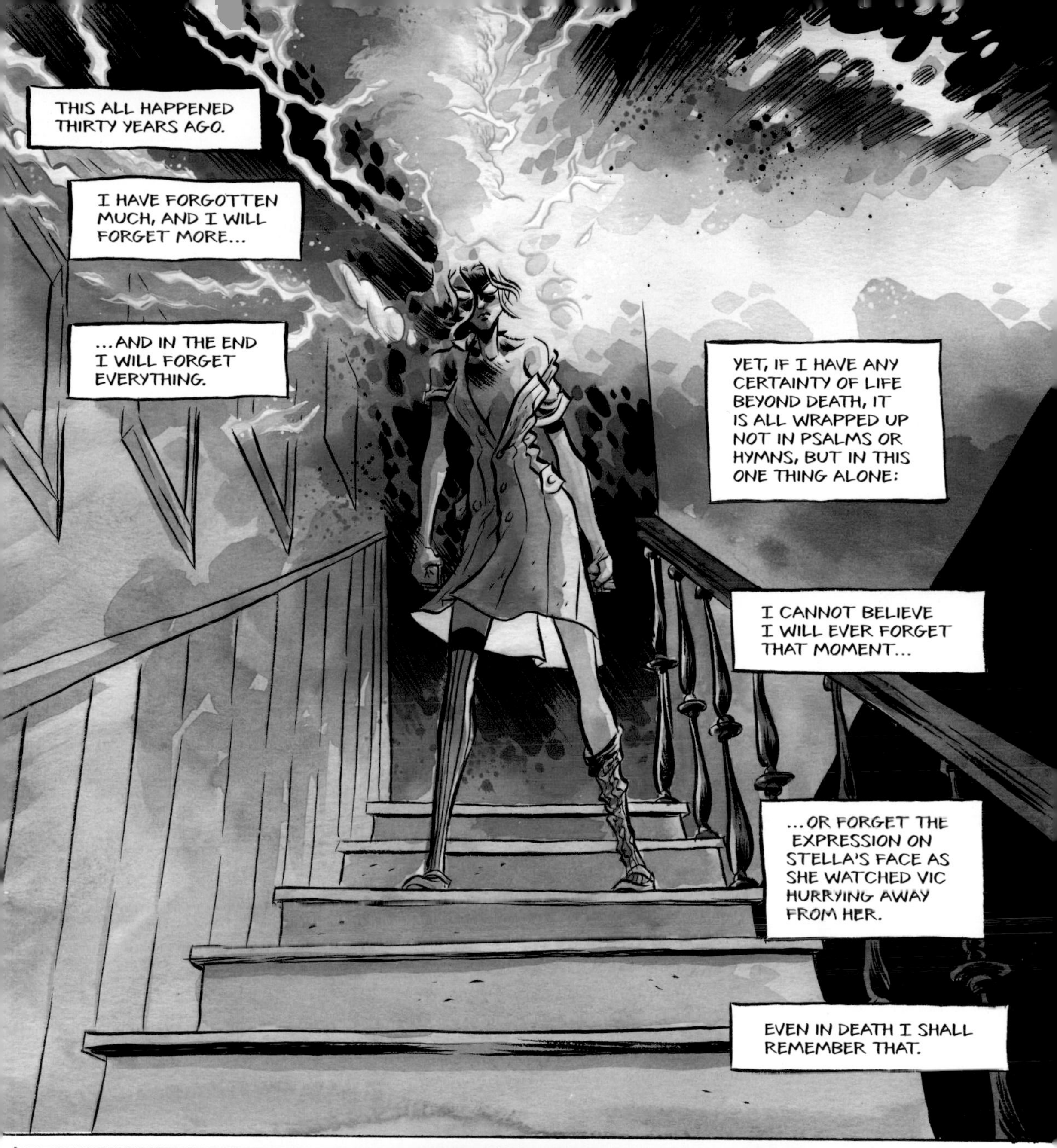
THIS ALL HAPPENED THIRTY YEARS AGO.
I HAVE FORGOTTEN MUCH, AND I WILL FORGET MORE...
...AND IN THE END I WILL FORGET EVERYTHING.
YET, IF I HAVE ANY CERTAINTY OF LIFE BEYOND DEATH, IT IS ALL WRAPPED UP NOT IN PSALMS OR HYMNS, BUT IN THIS ONE THING ALONE:
I CANNOT BELIEVE I WILL EVER FORGET THAT MOMENT...
...OR FORGET THE EXPRESSION ON STELLA'S FACE AS SHE WATCHED VIC HURRYING AWAY FROM HER.
EVEN IN DEATH I SHALL REMEMBER THAT.

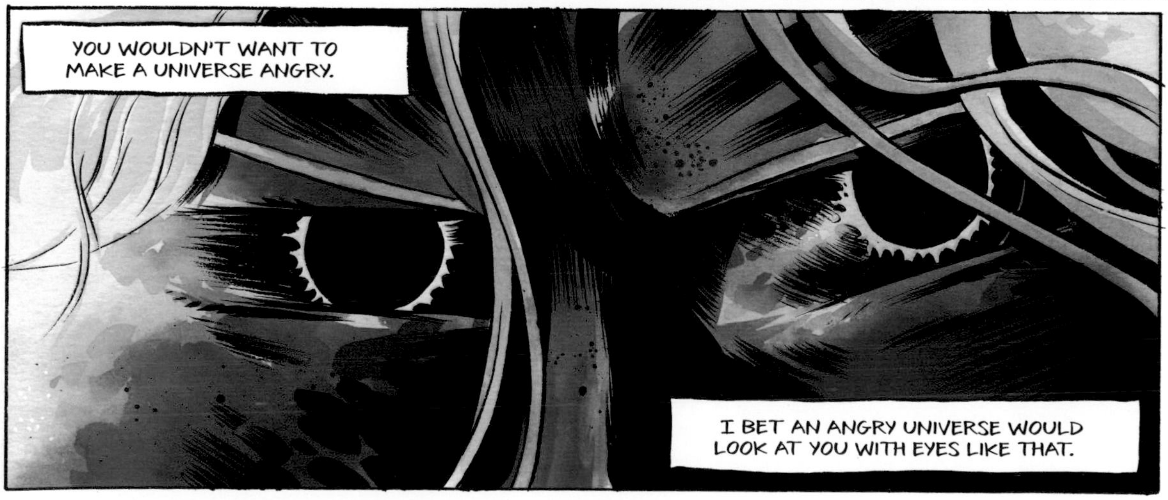
YOU WOULDN'T WANT TO MAKE A UNIVERSE ANGRY.
I BET AN ANGRY UNIVERSE WOULD LOOK AT YOU WITH EYES LIKE THAT.

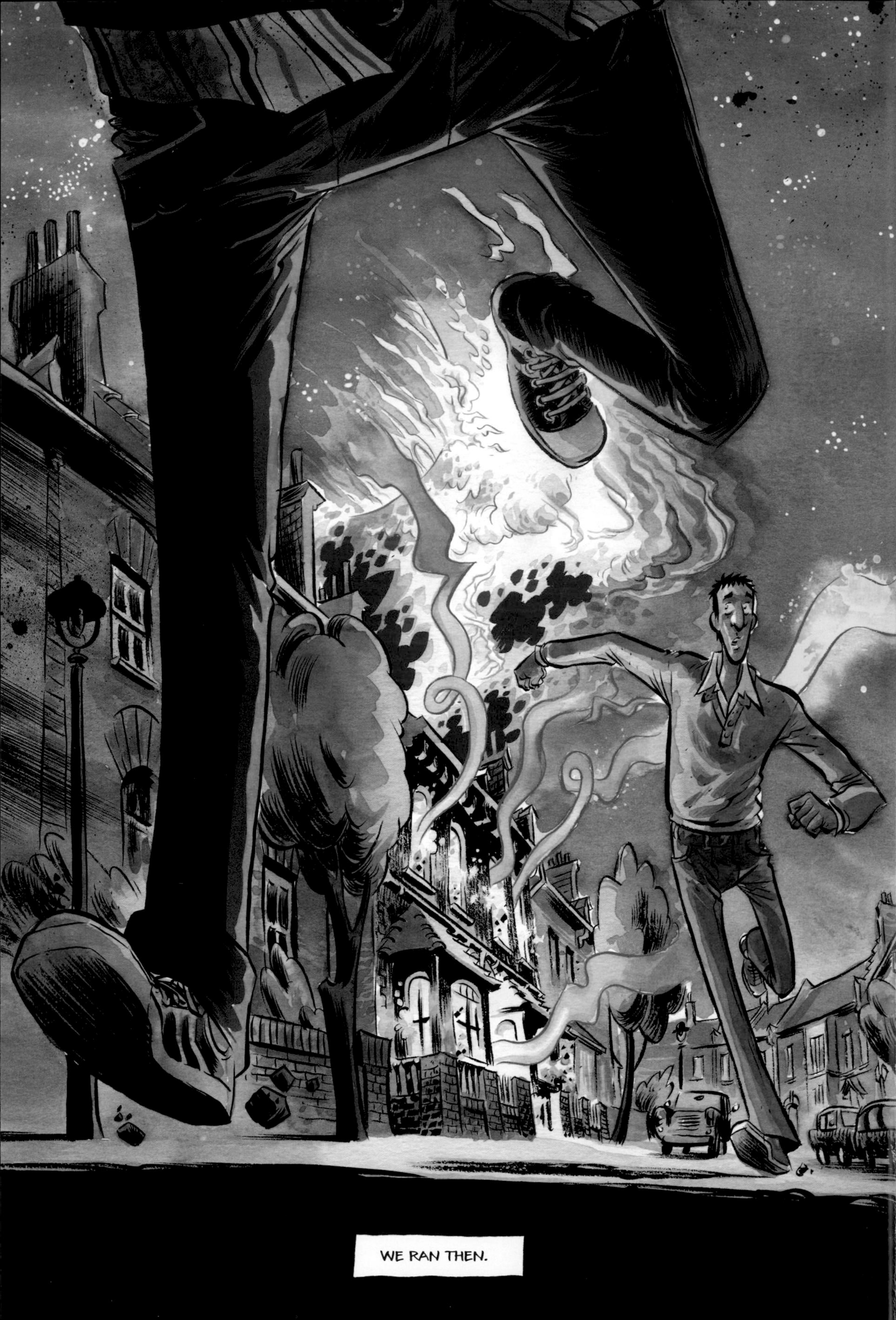
WE RAN THEN.

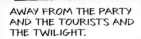

AWAY FROM THE PARTY AND THE TOURISTS AND THE TWILIGHT.

AS IF A LIGHTNING STORM WERE ON OUR HEELS: A MAD HELTER-SKELTER DASH DOWN THE CONFUSION OF STREETS.

WE DID NOT LOOK BACK.

WE DID NOT STOP UNTIL WE COULD NOT BREATHE.

UNF--

SHE--

SHE WASN'T A--

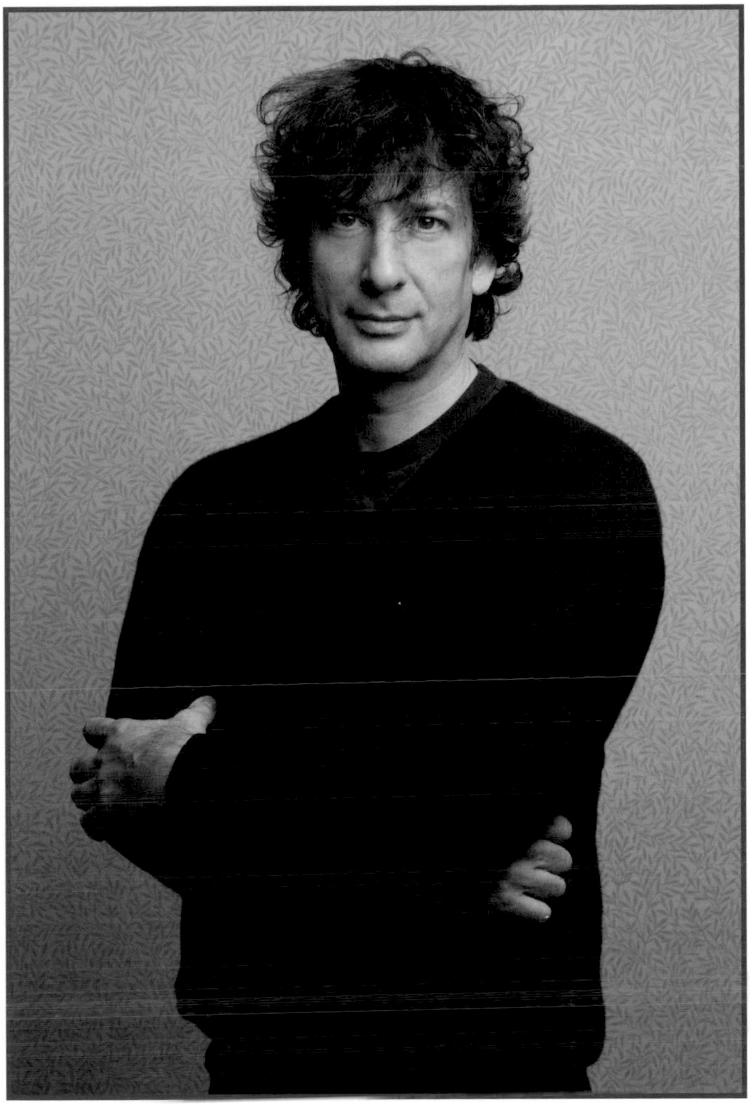

Photo by Kimberly Butler

NEIL GAIMAN

Neil Gaiman is the celebrated author of books, graphic novels, short stories, and films for readers of all ages.

Some of his most notable titles include the groundbreaking #1 *New York Times* bestselling *Sandman* comics series (which garnered nine Eisner Awards and the World Fantasy Award for Best Short Story); *The Graveyard Book* (the first book ever to win both the Newbery and Carnegie medals); *American Gods* (which will soon be released as a television show in the US); and *The Ocean at the End of the Lane,* the UK's National Book Award 2013 Book of the Year.

The film adaptation of *How to Talk to Girls at Parties* (directed by John Cameron Mitchell) will be in theaters in 2017.

Born in the UK, Neil now lives in the US with his wife, the musician and writer Amanda Palmer, and their son Anthony.

FÁBIO MOON & GABRIEL BÁ

Fábio Moon and Gabriel Bá are twin brothers born in 1976 in São Paulo, Brazil, where they live to this day. They have been telling stories in comic book form for over fifteen years, and their work has been published in twelve languages.

In 2007 they received their first Eisner Award nomination, for *De:Tales*, and the following year they won three Eisners for their work on *5*, *The Umbrella Academy*, and *Sugarshock!* Their 2010 limited series and magnum opus, *Daytripper*, garnered Eisner, Harvey, and Eagle awards, and went on to achieve great international acclaim through subsequent collections of the work.

The twins' most recent graphic novel, *Two Brothers*, has been touted as both "another masterpiece" and "a feat of bravura visual storytelling." When not at the drawing board, the Brazilian wonder twins continue to travel around the world, sharing their great love for comics.